CRIME'S NEMESIS

CRIME'S NEMESIS

LUKE S. MAY

CRIMINOLOGIST

COACHWHIP PUBLICATIONS

Landisville, Pennsylvania

CONTENTS

INTRODUCTION

When an individual commits a crime, he pits his wits and his chances of escape against life itself, every phase of it. Sometimes it would even seem that the criminal is shadowed by a sort of Nemesis provided by Fate to guard against those elements of society that would destroy civilization and life itself.

Though this metaphysical concept may appear to be a concession to superstition, a recognition of supermundane influences in the affairs of men of which we know nothing, no one who has long been in contact with criminals and their fate can escape the thought that subtle elements are at work that eventually trip up the most clever of criminals.

Call it coincidence if you will, or cause and effect, the fact remains that insignificant trifles of which the criminal has no knowledge and over which he has no control, often reveal the perpetrator of the so-called "perfect" crime.

Events that occurred months or perhaps years prior to the crime, unknown to the criminal, may bring themselves into play. A passing stranger, a bit of hair or fibre left at the scene of the crime, the sudden fall of rain, a flash of lightning, an unexpected thaw, or any other element of nature may contribute to the criminal's detection. A bit of foreign matter under a finger nail, blood in the pores of the skin, characteristics typical of a certain vocation—all such trifles are used to bring down the vengeance of the law upon the head of the criminal.

The successful criminologist has no illusions about himself, despite the superman that fiction depicts. He lays no claim to psychic powers of clairvoyance. And yet, he must be more clever than the criminal. The criminologist often fights a battle of wits with diabolical cunning. His knowledge of life and men must be immense; his powers of logic and deduction, acutely developed. His must be a thirst for knowledge in every field. His power of observation is usually a gift. Still, he is human, very human. His best allies are life and the criminal himself.

No crime is committed without leaving a trail to the perpetrator. There is always a clue. True, the criminologist may not detect it in every case, but it is there. Modern crime detection methods and the marvelous developments in the scientific detective laboratories of today bring stupendous odds against the criminal.

It is the purpose of this book to reveal these methods, bring them into the light of day that they may warn the potential criminal of the inevitable fate that sooner or later awaits every felon. Aside from the exaggerations of fiction, laymen have been given very little opportunity to observe the backstage operations of crime detection. Even though wide publicity may attend a famous case, the part played by the detective or criminologist is not properly shown on the public stage—the courtroom. How a crime is detected and the criminal apprehended is usually of no legal importance. Hence, even the criminal is ignorant of the many factors that brought him to justice.

The traditional secrecy involved in criminal detection, often necessary, has been reflected in an unnecessary reticence on the part of the criminologist to discuss his methods. I believe this to be a mistake. After all, the best deterrent of crime is fear of punishment. Of course, after a crime is committed the penal code should be redemptive as well as punitive in its purpose. It is fear of retribution that keeps many people out of jail.

Hence, it is the purpose of this volume to reveal the so-called mysteries of criminology, that all may count the chances before they launch out on a career of crime.

True it is that, for the moment, crime seems to be in the ascendant, and many criminals might seem to be immune to punishment. That is largely an illusion, though it is true that in this country there is a crying need for more man-power—trained men who have the talent and knowledge to combat crime adequately. The volume rather than the nature of crime is the challenging element.

Though the criminal takes every possible advantage of scientific discovery, so also does the criminologist, and more methodically. Criminology is a lifelong development, a lifelong study, and should be a lifelong profession, approached and followed with the same thoroughness that marks the medical profession, for example.

The writer, for instance, has spent a quarter of a century in the work of criminology, beginning at the age of seventeen years. Since then I have been compelled to study at least the rudiments of almost every science and of mechanical and electrical engineering, delve into all of the professions, and study the different types of society. Criminology demands much, but there is nothing superhuman about it. Much of this work, especially its application to crime problems, was, of necessity, original; for science has only recently become the handmaiden of the criminologist. When I opened a scientific detective laboratory, it was one of the first of its kind in the United States, with few if any precedents to follow.

The science of crime detection has advanced marvelously since the days of Vidocq, who first established an organized detective bureau in Paris at the beginning of the last century. Vidocq's success lay largely in his own criminal experience. He was a typical stool pigeon, chosen on the theory that "it takes a thief to catch a thief." His colleagues were all notorious criminals who turned against their fellows. He soon reverted to type and spent his last days in prison. In 1817 the French discontinued recruiting police officers from the ranks of criminals, and they have built up a crime detection institution in the Sureté that ranks with Scotland Yard in its terror to the underworld.

Modern scientific criminology had its genesis among many famous personalities of world-wide renown. Hans Gross of Prague is probably considered by American students of criminology as the outstanding disciple of science applied to criminal investigation. To the layman, Dr. Bertillon of Paris, who devised the anthropometric system of identification known as the Bertillon system, stands out as one of those making vast contributions to modern criminology.

The name which stands out preeminently among the pioneers in the study of criminology as a whole is that of Professor Lombroso. While many of Lombroso's theories are today discredited by profound students of criminology, his great contribution to this science was in drawing attention to the possibilities for studying the criminal class.

The same thing in some respects might be said of Dr. Bertillon, whose method of identification known as the Bertillon system has now become obsolete. However, many of Bertillon's exploits in the scientific investigation of crime outrival those of Sherlock Holmes, the figment of Conan Doyle's imagination. Without disparaging progressive police officers of all nations, I believe that the writings of Conan Doyle have done more than any other one thing to stimulate active interest in the scientific and analytical investigation of crime. All of these men helped introduce a fundamentally new technique in crime detection.

Prior to this the chief weapon of the detective involved the factors of motive and opportunity. These elements are still very useful at times. The criminal is traced backward from the crime, beginning with possible motive and opportunity to commit it. It often involved examining all suspects, and by the process of elimination fixing the guilt upon the most likely victim. Extracting a confession was usually the last step in this type of approach.

On the other hand, there is the method that begins with the crime, places every bit of physical evidence under scientific scrutiny, and by deduction visualizes the crime and the criminal, extending this conception toward the possible perpetrator.

The former method depends largely on verbal testimony; the latter, on the testimony of visible tangible evidence on the physical plane.

Dr. Hans Gross, the famous anthropologist and criminologist of Prague, ably describes this distinction:

> The correct sketch be it ever so simple, a microscopic slide, a deciphered correspondence, a photograph of a person or object, a tattooing, a restored piece of burned paper, a careful survey, a thousand more material things, are all examples of incorruptible evidence, disinterested and enduring testimony from which mistaken, inaccurate, and biased perceptions, as well as evil intention, perjury, and unlawful coöperation are excluded. As the science of criminal investigation proceeds, oral testimony falls behind and the importance of realistic proof advances.

The laboratory has made this new approach in crime detection a formidable weapon, but the older methods of espionage, neighborhood gossip, the informant, the motive, and opportunity are still, and always will be, used effectively in criminal cases.

The chief value of physical evidence, scientifically analyzed and presented, is not only the aid it gives the police in apprehending the criminal, but also the irrefutable evidence it offers the court. The criminal may confess, but the prosecutor must prove the facts of confession!

The advance made by science in crime detection has been vast. The imprint of a hard substance on a softer, such as a knife cut on a twig or a revolver barrel on a bullet, as seen under a magnascope and pictured by a photomicrograph, has been the undoing of countless criminals. The study of the criminal mind through psychiatry has been invaluable. *Modus operandi* is another modern development, and its combination with finger-printing makes life miserable for the habitual criminal.

How these elements are actually applied in real crime cases will be analyzed in the following pages.

It is, perhaps, unnecessary to emphasize that these cases are true stories of actual crimes that were once mysteries. Yet, so much has been written under the guise of true detective tales that is really

pure figment of the imagination that the distinction is not imper-
tinent.

The fiction story that makes no pretense of being based on actual
happenings provides splendid recreational reading, but cannot
fulfill the mission of this volume. Truth and accuracy alone can
give that authenticity for which we have striven, although in many
instances we use fictitious names.

A conscious effort was made to avoid the highly colored, sen-
sational narrative that exaggerates the morbid and gruesome.
Never has accuracy been sacrificed for dramatic suspense. Usually, this is unnecessary, for the experience of human conflict and
intrigue that is the lot of the criminologist need no trimmings to
make thrilling tales of poignant emotion and stirring adventure.

Likewise, in this volume I have tried to avoid burdensome details that would interest only the professional technician. In other
words, it is not a technical treatise in which laboratory findings
are allowed to overshadow the human story of love, passion, intrigue, devotion, frailty, loss, defeat, and victory that is the warp
and woof of every crime.

1
THERE IS ALWAYS A CLUE

If the detective depended alone upon super-mentality or a psychic sense to solve a crime mystery, he would soon be floundering in a morass of question marks.

If he went to the scene of a crime expecting a clue to stare him in the face, his lot would be much easier than it is.

Most crimes are mysteries for a time. A few are never solved. Yet, it is a truism in criminology that every crime leaves a trail to the perpetrator. This trail is sometimes overlooked, sometimes long and tortuous, but it is there. Whether such spoors are the result of the influence of a universal law protecting humanity against destructive elements, or whether they result from human imperfection unable to control or anticipate every contingency, it is impossible to say. The murderer not only violates the rights of his victim, but strikes with his deadly weapon at the most vital principle of Nature—life itself. Sometimes it does seem that metaphysical forces are pitted against the criminal who defies all laws of harmonious existence.

Still the detective cannot depend entirely on such elements that lay bare a clue. He must use the means at his disposal—a well-ordered system of investigation. If the criminal or the criminally disposed realized how minutely thorough such investigations are, they would think twice or thrice before committing a felony. It is the purpose of this chapter to reveal a definite system of procedure by which a skilled criminologist goes about solving a crime mystery.

Not all detectives use identical methods, nor are all methods applicable to every case; but systematic procedure there must be to insure a reasonable percentage of success. The method outlined is the result of a quarter of a century of experience in crime detection, the fruit of a minute analysis of over one thousand cases successfully solved. In actual practice, ninety-seven per cent of the cases in which it has been employed have been unraveled.

In basic principle the work of the detective, the man who does the field investigation, is merely an evolved and refined version of the tactics employed by the primitive savage in tracing and stalking an enemy through a forest jungle. An almost invisible mark on the ground, a broken twig, a fallen leaf, the embers of a camp fire are all telltale marks that guide the way. In other words, espionage, used in its broadest sense, is the foundation upon which the modern detective works. The scientific developments in the laboratory have proved a marvelous weapon against the criminal, and yet the human factors of observation, logical deductions, and knowledge of men are still the groundwork of criminology.

It is on this premise that the system described is built. It is outlined fully enough to give the layman a conception of what the criminal is up against, though in this treatise we make no pretense of a technical exposition for the professional investigator, the specific scientific principles for making a complete investigation of a mysterious murder being fully outlined in my manual, *Scientific Murder Investigation* (1934).

Each detective or operative carries in his pocket a small notebook containing methods of detection procedure for every known crime. In these outlines nothing is overlooked. No possible source of information can be forgotten in the excitement of the crime. Like an invisible web the investigation reaches out from the scene of the crime and sweeps every possible bit of information and evidence into its meshes, where it is sorted, classified, and analyzed to find the clue that leads to the criminal. If this work is done thoroughly, the criminal will rarely, if ever, escape suspicion. Then begins apprehension and conviction, which is another thing.

For example, glancing through the detective's notebook, we find an outline of procedure in a murder case. Each point is numbered as follows:

1. Who is the person murdered? Friends, habits, finances, enemies?

2. What is the apparent motive, if any is shown? This may not be the actual motive.

3. Who saw the victim last?

4. Time the crime was committed; fix to the minute if possible.

5. Find out all persons who are living at, or working at, or who have visited the scene of the crime or person murdered for two weeks previous or longer.

6. Question everyone in the vicinity of any persons who may have been seen leaving the scene of the crime. Did they hear any sounds, see any strange people, or do they know of any information that might in any way show the guilty person? Go through this thoroughly and leave out no one.

7. Question and get names and addresses of all employees now employed near or in the neighborhood; also those who have been discharged.

8. Make a thorough search for signs of struggle; see if anything is missing: jewelry, papers, records, pictures, tools. Have there been any instruments or tools of any description or nature left at the scene of the crime? Go over this matter very thoroughly with someone who is familiar with the premises—and leave out nothing. This has been the means of working out many great cases and is often overlooked by experienced detectives.

9. Has there been anything destroyed: records, pictures, instruments, jewelry, furniture? If so, what is the motive for it?

10. Who reported the murder? Where were they for twelve hours previous? How did they learn of it? What aroused

their suspicion? Are they reliable? What is their theory of motive?

11. Examine entrance and exit to scene of crime: Was the person familiar with premises? Did murderer come and go hurriedly or was he or she there some time? What method was used by the murderer to kill the victim?

12. Get theories advanced by responsible and irresponsible persons who are interested in the crime, and check them carefully. Who would be benefited by the victim's death? Who would lose? Get their names and addresses.

When a detective has diligently run the gamut of these points of investigation, he will have more clues than he can immediately follow up, provided he is a trained detective. Such investigation will ordinarily work out the most mystifying cases. A similar, though varying, type of procedure is followed in every type of crime. There is little escape for the criminal.

A classic example of the system applied to murder is that of the Thomas Clinton case. Thomas Clinton was a student attending the University of Utah. He lived in Salt Lake City with his mother, sister, and two brothers. One noon in 1909 he went home to lunch, and a few minutes after he had entered the home, he came running out screaming. A few staggering steps and he fell dead. A street-car conductor who saw this episode reported the crime. The victim had been shot several times.

Some curiosity seekers and neighbors overran the place destroying what little marks of evidence had been left by the murderer. I was called into the case by a friend of the family.

The home was situated on a hilly place and the house itself on a level spot, with an incline down to the street level. In the back of the house, extending about one hundred feet, was a sheer drop of over ten or twelve feet, and then a further incline. A number of large residences were on each side. I made note of this terrain and the surroundings, not knowing, of course, what part, if any, this would play in the solution of the mystery. Such things are all a matter of routine.

All the neighbors were visited, and it was discovered that a woman living three houses away had seen a man run out of the house directly after the shooting and disappear down over the bank.

Carrying the investigation into the house of the murdered victim, we found a revolver with three shells exploded. It seemed quite obvious that this was the gun that had fired the fatal shots.

Having established the gun that fired the shot, we yet had to find the man who had pulled the death-dealing trigger. Questioning the relatives of the victim, we found that the gun belonged to a brother who had left it on the dresser that morning. As a matter of routine this brother was quickly and entirely eliminated by an absolute alibi and by an absence of motive as he loved his brother dearly.

He was at his University classes at the time of the crime and could not have been implicated. This fact was further supported by an apparent motive of burglary as some money had been rifled from his dresser drawer.

The case seemed an absolute cul-de-sac. There appeared to be no real clue except a footprint which was found over the bank at the back where some one had jumped. A fairly good description could be obtained from this as the trained detective can judge the height and weight from the footprints left in soft ground by a running man.

In following out the investigation called for in Paragraph 8 of the outline, a surprising development occurred. A brother of the deceased and I went over the entire house to note any disarrangement, looking for missing articles or anything left by the murderer.

It all seemed fruitless. As a last resort we went into the basement. There I stumbled on a handsaw that lay on the floor.

"You really ought to hang up that saw where it belongs before it gets rusty from the dampness," I told him casually. I have a fondness for tools that expressed itself in this rather inconsequential episode. Any number of police officers, including the local chief of detectives, had walked over the saw and given it no heed whatever, as evidenced by the heel marks and dirt on its surface.

But my chance remark proved one of those trifles that seem almost providential in significance.

Clinton's grief-stricken eyes had never noticed it before. "What saw?" He picked it up. "Why, that's not our saw. We haven't a saw on the place."

"Are you positive?"

"Absolutely. We have no saw like that."

"The murderer left it here."

Clinton looked at me incredulously. "What would a burglar want with an old cross-cut saw?"

"I don't know, but who else could have left it?"

I was confident in my surmise. Reviewing Paragraph 6 in the outline developed the fact that a man carrying a saw had been seen in the vicinity a short time before the shooting.

"You bet I remember a man with a saw," the street-car conductor told the Chief of Police. "He was rather a foreign-looking chap with small beady black eyes. He was undecided where to get off."

Questioning produced a good description of the man.

"Where did he get on your car?"

"Let me see." The conductor considered a moment. "He gave me a Murray transfer."

The trail was getting warmer. Interviewing all the conductors on the Murray line revealed the fact that a man carrying a saw had ridden on the Murray line, but had not been seen since the time of the murder. This bit of evidence seemed conclusive that we were on the right track.

Tracing back, city detectives learned where this man usually got on the Murray cars. Inquiry among neighbors led them to the home of the owner of the saw, who had loaned it to the man who proved to be the murderer.

He was a man who had a job to saw some wood. On the day of the murder he had gone to the wrong address—the Clinton home instead of another. There he had found doors unlocked and nobody at home. The temptation to enter and rifle the place had been too strong to resist. He was not an habitual criminal; the natural instinct of acquisition, for the moment, was not controlled by the higher principles of property rights and social values. The primitive instinct was stronger than the man's moral fibre. He was tried and convicted, but maintained innocence up to a few hours before he was executed.

Acquisition is a human trait that is praiseworthy, rightly applied. "Vice is frequently only virtue in excess," says Bernard Hollander.[1]

Entering the basement door, the man left his saw on the floor. Surprised while rifling the dresser drawer by the boy coming home to lunch, the man was overcome by fear. He seized the revolver near by, fired at the boy, and then fled through the rear door.

It is evident that not all of the twelve points in the murder investigation have a bearing on every case, but it is certain that one or more of these channels of inquiry will reveal facts that prove the undoing of the perpetrator of almost every crime. The carefully planned crime is usually much easier to unravel than the accidental crime, such as the one described. The clever criminal who tries to perform a perfect crime uses known principles of reason and logic. His is a conscious effort involving habits of thinking well known to psychologists. His acts are predictable, and the various steps in the crime are easily traced after a clue has been found. On the other hand, the accidental crime usually has neither rhyme nor reason. Anything can happen at the spur of the moment. Often the element of motive is entirely lacking.

The Clinton case also presents another interesting phase of criminology, that of making opportunities for the criminal. Had the door not been unlocked in the basement, it is quite doubtful whether the murderer would have entered. While "love laughs at locksmiths," many men are in the penitentiary because of locks; and by the same token many are outside.

If there is one faculty more valuable to a detective than any other, it is a talent for penetrating and interpreting the thought processes of all types of people. A blacksmith committing a crime would act and think differently from a college professor. A gangster thinks differently from a ribbon salesman. Not only must the

---

[1] *The Psychology of Misconduct, Vice, and Crime*, by Bernard Hollander, M.D.

detective understand psychology in its broad aspects, but he must be thoroughly conversant with class or social psychology in order to understand desires, motives, habits, and behavior patterns of all types of people. To visualize the manner in which a crime was committed, its motive and purpose, it is necessary for the detective to assume mentally a dual role—that of the criminal and that of the victim. Success in this respect has solved many a murder mystery.

2
Meeting Doom in the Laboratory

Many crime mysteries are solved merely by the intelligent use of ordinary human faculties. The detective discovers a motive. By carefully eliminating the persons who would have an interest in committing the crime, or who would have had an opportunity to commit the crime, the suspects are narrowed down to one or perhaps more individuals. Ingenuity in tracing back the steps leading up to the crime, determining the whereabouts of suspects at the time the crime was committed, and other means, may lead to the arrest of the alleged culprit. Then may follow a confession.

Many desperate criminals, and perhaps some innocent victims of circumstances, have been brought to the gallows by such means. Through it is woven the web of circumstantial evidence that has been known to defeat the end of justice. Even a confession is not to be relied upon. In the case of homicide the court of law insists that the facts of the confession must be proved to the satisfaction of the jury.

Unless a confession reveals facts of incriminating evidence that can be verified, it is worthless in the case of murder. And many confessions are known to be false. It may seem unreasonable that an individual is willing to flirt with the gallows and endure confinement in jail unnecessarily. It is not. Sometimes a wife, sweetheart, lover, or parent may confess to a crime committed by a loved one so as to permit the loved one to escape. At the trial the one who has confessed can present an absolute alibi and gain release, while in the meantime the real criminal has escaped beyond the hand of the law.

Sometimes such a bogus confession is the result of mental ab-
normality that craves the public limelight at all costs. At other times
the object of such a confession is a total enigma. An officer in
Pocatello, Idaho, was murdered by a negro. Newspapers furnished
the public with all the details. A little later a negro by the name of
Frank Allen confessed to the crime. He had all his facts straight,
for he had read them in the newspapers. It all seemed very plausible. I took his fingerprints. His record was checked, and it was
found that at the time the murder was committed he had been in
prison. In the vernacular of the street, he was simply "cracked."
Sometimes an individual will falsely confess to a small crime to
avoid the consequences of a greater. He will hide away in jail till
the smoke blows away.

Unimpeachable physical evidence avoids the pitfalls of circumstantial evidence, of hearsay, and bogus confessions. That is why
the scientific laboratory, with its test tubes and its precision instruments, has proved of such transcendent value to the criminologist.
Seeming miracles are performed almost every day.

No longer is the traditional detective confined to crime detection. The geologist, the zoologist, the chemist, the psychologist,
the pathologist, the engineer, and in fact every expert craftsman
play parts in the modern man-hunt.

Nothing is too insignificant to focus the attention of the scientific criminal investigator. Instruments, dust, weapons, dynamite,
letters, hair, fibres, the fur of animals, jewelry, stains are just a
few items that have brought criminals to justice. In one case to
which I was called a lone match was the clue that unraveled a most
baffling crime.

It happened in an Idaho mining town. The wife of an official of
a big mine was awakened at one o'clock in the morning with a feeling that some one was in the room. She could hear the breathing
of something; then she felt the hot breath on her face. She started
to scream when her throat was clutched in the bearlike grasp of a
huge rough hand. She struggled with all her strength, but in vain,
against this brutal attack; suddenly there was a clattering of metal
on stone outside. A miner going home from work, it was afterwards

learned, had slipped and banged his lunch bucket on the rocks lining the trail. Her assailant having committed his fiendish assault became excited. He tried to get out. In the dim light of the starlit night, from the inside, the window and door looked identical, for the upper part of the door had just such a glass pane as the window. The burglar became confused, mistaking the window for the door. On such things does fate hang. He fumbled around a long minute, trying to find the door knob. At last he struck a match, threw it carelessly on the floor, and rushed out.

The woman never saw the intruder's face and hence no description was available. Local officials made an investigation, but decided there wasn't a single clue, except possibly fingerprints.

I was called in. I went over the premises as thoroughly as I could. What the sheriff said apparently was true—there seemed not a single clue, not even a fingerprint, for these had been obliterated.

"Then the burglar lit a match, and—" the woman of the house repeated her story to me. She had explained about the match to all the officials.

"Where?" A clue at last.

"Right over there by the window, I think," she answered, surprised at my interest.

A chair was tilted against the wall near the window she indicated.

"That's where a friend of mine was sitting just a few hours before the robbery," the mine official explained. "We've left everything in the room, just as it was."

"What did you and your friend do that evening?" I asked.

"He stayed until about eleven o'clock," the man replied; "then he went with me on an inspection trip through the mine. While he was here we just talked—and smoked a lot. Look at the matches we threw on the floor."

I gathered up the matches. There were thirteen in all. Twelve were grooved in the shafts. The thirteenth was round and crimped on the end.

"This one with the crimp is the one we want," I remarked to the sheriff.

"Say, I can get you a million just like that," the sheriff replied. His skepticism was thinly veneered with a laugh.

"Maybe a million similar to it, but not one just like it. There are no two things in the world exactly alike, under the microscope."

"Well, what of it?"

"We will see."

The match was placed under a powerful microscope. A tiny speck, invisible to the naked eye, caught my attention. It was a fibre, but it didn't match in texture or color any of the hundreds of samples in the laboratory. Presumably, it was from the lining of the pocket in which the match had been carried. Whatever it was, the significant thing was that it was probably from some cloth of foreign manufacture.

The match was rotated very carefully under the microscope. Here was a tiny stain—grease or machine oil! And embedded in the oil was a speck of coal dust.

Another turn, and the infinitesimal glint of a crystal of metal shot up the beam through the glass. No—on closer study, the crystal was composed of two metals; microchemical analysis proved it to be brass and iron. It was probably a filing, such as is found where brazing is done.

Four days had elapsed since the burglary.

Calling at the engine-rooms of the seven mines in the vicinity, we learned that a cylinder head on one of the engines in a certain mine had blown and had been repaired by brazing just five days before.

I asked to talk to the man who had done the filing on the brazing work. He was brought in—a husky foreigner.

The man visibly paled as the sheriff searched him. Under the man's overalls was found another suit. It was European in cut and odd in texture. In one of the pockets we found several matches— round ones and crimped in the end. I took several threads from the lining of the pocket. Then I proceeded to give him a careful manicure with a special instrument, saving the dirt from under the nails.

Under the microscope, the fibres compared exactly with the one on the match found at the scene of the crime; and embedded in the dirt under the nails were filings of brass and iron. There were tiny grease stains and coal dust on the inside of the man's pocket.

Faced with this damaging evidence, the man confessed to the crime. Some might say that we might have found the same evidence on some other man in the camp.

There were more than seven hundred men in this mining town. But if there were seven hundred thousand, I still would know that we were right, for I had ten factors brought together in a combination which, according to the "law of probabilities," cannot happen more than once in several million times!

The law of probabilities is as real as the law of gravitation. The more factors—not theories—you have combined toward a certain conclusion, the more definite becomes the conclusion.

That is why the criminal is usually caught in the end. Always he is working against infinite possibilities for probable slip-ups, and no human brain ever existed that could go up against the infinite in any form and come out a winner. This universal law seems to be a watching Nemesis that dogs the footsteps of the criminal.

Science has become a marvelous handmaiden of the criminologist. Invisible physical evidence is almost as good for identification purposes as a photograph of the crime in action.

A hair from your head, for instance, isn't like any other hair in the world—any more than one tree is like any other tree in every single particular. There may be many points of similarity, but somewhere in the structure there is the variation that means you— and nobody else.

In fact, a human hair can tell the scientific criminologist a great many interesting things. Sometimes it is possible to get a fairly good description of an individual based on probabilities. If the hair roots are intact, the age of the person from whose head they came may be determined approximately by dissolving the roots in a strong alkali. The younger the person, the more easily the roots are dissolved. A child's hair dissolves almost immediately; in the hair of a mature person there is considerable resistance, ranging up to several hours in really old people. Hair also varies in pigmentation with age. Children's hair has a small medulla or core. Racial characteristics can be determined from the hair. The importance of such evidence will be dealt with in a later chapter.

Not only actual physical properties of your body, such as general appearance, complexion, size, weight, and fingerprints, but everything about your person reveals an interesting tale to him who understands.

If you were to submit yourself to a laboratory examination, you would indeed be startled by the uncanny things discovered about you. Examining the palms of your hands would reveal traces of objects you have handled during the preceding half-hour. The lining in your pockets would tell what had been contained in them for a considerable period. After an examination of the prints of your shoes on the floor, the small particles of dust adhering to the leather might tell where you had been during the day—whether on a pavement, a dusty road, in the garden, or on a carpet and what kind of carpet.

If you had visited the barber earlier in the day, that would be easily determined. Bits of powder on your face might give a clue as to what barber you visited, provided he used a special brand. If you had a hair-cut, this would be revealed by bits of hair on your coat bearing the unmistakable marks of scissors. Under the microscope they would look like logs cut with a jagged saw. Examining the bits of dust adhering to the wax of the inner ear might reveal your vocation. If you were a miller, particles of flour dust would be discovered. Coal dust might indicate that you worked with coal, either as a miner or as a fireman; clay, that you worked in a brickyard, etc.

All such minutiae may have the most vital bearing on a crime mystery. The detective visiting the scene of a crime goes prepared to recognize and preserve such trifles of evidence that seem to mean nothing at all. He carries with him a roll of paper in which to wrap all manner of objects that may have a bearing on the crime. Bullets are wrapped in a special brand of filter paper and placed in sealed boxes after they are carefully marked and dated with the aid of a pocket microscope. A piece of paper on the floor at the scene of the crime may look like any other waste paper. The detective carefully picks it up with clean and sterile tweezers so that his own fingerprints may not mar any previous impressions. This is carefully sealed in an envelope. Papers can be put through a process of developing just like the negative of a photograph. It may reveal a great deal more than a fingerprint.

Sometimes it is advisable to gather dust at the scene of the crime. To do this the operator places several thicknesses of clean muslin or linen on the nozzle of a vacuum cleaner. It is then sucked up into the muslin pocket so formed and thus preserved for examination in the laboratory.

Even a charred paper that has been burned may be preserved between two glass plates. Writing that may have been on the paper will often be as clearly revealed as before burning.

In one case a blank sheet of paper found under suspicious circumstances resisted ordinary efforts to develop invisible ink writing. The paper was then photographed with infra-red light and the proper infra-red sensitive materials. This experiment developed a cryptogram—a code message that revealed the plans for a wholesale jailbreak. The perpetrators were caught red-handed.

Footprints in soil, and the tread of an automobile tire, are easily preserved by means of *moulage*, a plaster cast, or perspective and metric photography.

It is minute attention to such details that has unraveled a great many crime mysteries.

The microscope and the test tube are marvelous aids in such investigations. Even the ordinary camera is a part of the criminologist's equipment. It often sees more than the naked eye. A case comes to mind:

A suspect had been arrested in a stabbing affray. He was photographed, or "mugged" in the vernacular of the police. When I saw the picture, I noticed a dim outline across the man's shirt—as if the film had been dirty when the print was made.

I had the man photographed again. It was unlikely that two films would be identically defective. Again the outline showed up. To the naked eye the shirt seemed perfectly white and clean.

After this test I took the shirt itself and studied it. Tests showed that the dim outline was the remainder of a blood stain left after the shirt had been washed. This evidence, which seemed uncanny to the suspect, was sufficient to induce a complete confession.

The criminal is indeed faced with startling odds that mystify and confuse him. As a rule he is superstitious, and little wonder! His fear complex often makes him wilt quickly when confronted with evidence which to him seems like the hand of Fate, and who can say it is not?

3
TELLTALE FINGER MARKS

No one thing has interested the public in the work of tripping up criminals more than the finger marks they leave at the scene of the crime. Though a relatively new police method, finger-printing has become the most universally used means of criminal identification. Not only does such identification aid in apprehending and convicting an offender, but it tells the presiding judge whether it is a first offense or whether the prisoner at the bar is an old offender—a recidivist in the language of the court. Severity of penalty can be governed accordingly, varying from a minimum to a life imprisonment for the fourth offense in some states.

And it is all very simple.

Place a finger on any smooth or polished object. If it happens to be a dark object, such as a piece of furniture, go to your medicine chest and secure some sort of white powder, tooth powder, for example. Sprinkle this on the spot touched by your finger. After the surplus powder has been blown away, a clear impression of your fingerprint can be seen with the naked eye. If the object you touch is light in color, such as a piece of white china, the same results can be achieved by using a black powder—pulverized charcoal such as is taken for dyspepsia will serve.

The finger impression that you see belongs to you and to no other person in the world. Each finger has its own characteristic papillary lines, its peculiar ridge formation and pattern, it remains the same from birth to death, and even after death until putrefaction sets in. Though the tip of a finger may be worn smooth by pumice stone or acid, the characteristic pattern returns. These factors make the fingerprint an absolutely sure means of personal identification.

In my research study of fingerprints I have had occasion to examine fingers of people seven years after death; and where the embalming has been properly carried out, finger patterns are still intact, the same as in life. I have also noted that a seven-month stillborn babe's fingerprint pattern is clearly defined, and I have in my files the palm and foot impressions of many newly born babes taken in maternity hospitals for anxious mothers who had a fear that they might not get their own child.

The best manner which I have found to take a newly born infant's foot and palm prints is to take a clean watch glass, the convex surface of which will fit into the concave portion of the palm and the instep. Rub the palm and sole with olive oil, take up all surplus oil with a swab of gauze or cotton, wiping as dry as possible. The print is then impressed on the glass, taken to the laboratory, and developed with permanent powder. Most of the minute lines are so faint they can be seen only with a high-powered magnifying glass; however, when so viewed, all the intricacies and detail of pattern are clearly shown.

Let us refer again to your experiment with the tooth powder and pulverized charcoal. The criminal investigator goes a step farther. Instead of using crude methods as outlined above, the criminologist uses complex chemical formulas, black light, and other technical means to develop prints. He photographs such finger marks either at the scene of the crime or in the laboratory. These latent fingerprints are then used as an aid in apprehending or identifying suspects. More of this later.

The first systematized means of criminal identification was the Bertillon system, named after the famous French anthropologist, Alphonse Bertillon, who devised and perfected the system in 1882. It involved the measurement of certain parts of the body which remain unchanged during adult life. But it was far from perfect, though a decided advance over anything previously attempted. It could not be accurately applied to anyone under twenty-one years or over sixty years. Also its accuracy depended on the technique of the operator in making measurements. The difference between a "loose" and a "tight" measurement would be very marked.

At the present time the Bertillon system has been almost entirely displaced by some form of fingerprinting. Though ancients knew of the characteristic peculiarities of the fingerprint, it was not used as a means of criminal identification until a relatively few years ago. Sir William Herschel makes the statement that the ancient Chinese used the fingerprint as a countersignature on bank notes. Even before the criminologist made use of the fingerprint, Herschel himself had used it for seventeen years in his dealings with natives of India.

As is generally the case, it was a scientist who made the investigations that became the basis for fingerprinting as we now know it. Sir Francis Galton, a famous English scientist, in his study of heredity, established the fact that no two fingerprints are ever alike. Following up this established theory, Sir E. R. Henry, Assistant Commissioner of Metropolitan Police, London, devised a simple but comprehensive system of filing and classifying prints. That was in 1901. Two years later it was introduced into the Sing Sing prison of New York. The "Henry system" is now almost universally used, with many perfections by American and English authorities.

One of the first cases reported[1] in which the latent fingerprint led to the arrest of the criminal, is almost ludicrous in its crude technique.

Two men were found in possession of property under suspicious circumstances. When arrested they protested that they were merely transporting the property for a third party. Inquiry revealed that it had been stolen from a minister's home while he was away on a vacation. The men had removed the slates from the roof over the bathroom. They had let themselves down to the floor of the room by means of an open door. Carefully the investigators removed the seven-foot door from its hinges. Meticulously they wrapped it in paper and triumphantly placed it on a van to be transported to the

[1] *Criminal Investigation*, by Hans G. A. Gross.

town hall. There it was photographed, and comparison of fingerprints convicted the two men.

From that time to this fingerprints have played a major role in
discovering the perpetrators of crime. Sometimes, however, even
a clear fingerprint may confuse and dumbfound the investigator.
There was the case of Smith—we will disguise his identity under
that name.

He came home from the office as usual one night, and he had
either just stepped on the porch of the home or had opened the
front door when a shot rang out. He claimed that he had just put
his hand on the door knob. Some of the neighbors agreed with him,
but others thought he had had time to step inside when the shot
sounded.

At any rate, a few seconds later he came running out of the
house, shouting hysterically, "My wife has been killed! My wife has
been killed!"

The police were on the ground within a few minutes. By the
time they arrived the man was so hysterical he couldn't talk con-
nectedly, and many thought he knew more about the crime than
he would admit. Several neighbors heightened the excitement by
saying that they thought they had heard the man and his wife quar-
reling that very morning just before he went down to the office.

The body of the wife was found on the couch in the living room.
In the middle of her forehead was the fatal bullet wound. I was
called in consultation by the chief of police. I asked to see the gun
in the case.

"That's what stumps us," said the chief of police. "We can't find
any gun!"

Smith had been searched; the windows in the house were all
secured; and the back door was locked. Yet, somehow, the gun had
disappeared.

Excluding everyone but the officers, we searched the room. We
got around to the old-fashioned couch, and we pulled it out from
the wall. There was a soft thud; it was caused by the revolver drop-
ping to the floor,

"I suppose the theory is," one of the officers suggested cynically, "that she shot herself and then dropped the gun back of the couch!"

The husband's unverified story about his entrance, his demeanor, the reports of the quarrel, and every situation at the scene of the shooting pointed to his guilt. He was arrested.

My tests showed many of the woman's fingerprints on the gun—but only two of Smith's. The husband's fingerprints were on an odd place—just back of the shell chamber, as though he had grasped it with his thumb and forefinger with the hammer between his fingers. Only the finger tips were visible, indicating that the gun had been held very gingerly.

"As a matter of fact," I said to Smith, "didn't you hold it that way when you dropped it behind the couch?" The question took him by surprise.

He stared at me a moment with his reddened eyes before he said, "Yes!" Then he began to sob again, and I couldn't get any more out of him.

I removed the trigger from the gun. Across it were two prints, straight lines instead of the round circular lines usually found on the finger tips. They were the marks of the finger that had pulled the trigger.

They *almost* tallied with the lines on Smith's forefinger—but the fact remained that they did not tally. And the marks on the trigger were not those of Mrs. Smith's forefinger either! That I knew from the start, for it would have been impossible for her to pull the trigger with her forefinger and at the same time to hold the gun in such a way as to give the bullet the direction it had taken.

While I was handling the gun, the solution came to me suddenly. She *had* killed herself! And this is the way she did it. She had slipped her thumb through the trigger guard, and placed four fingers over the back of the handle. Just the way a woman would do it! The marks on the trigger and the lines of her thumb at the first joint tallied exactly.

But the gun behind the couch?

Smith threw light on that. I asked him why in the world he had put it there, and his reply was: "I don't know. I didn't even know I had done it until you reminded me I had."

Yet this subconscious act had almost incriminated him. The psychologist has a plausible explanation for the act. He was trying to shield his wife from the stigma of suicide, evidence that he really loved her. It merely emphasizes the fact that few can control emotions and acts under great stress and excitement. The detective must consider such unknown and unpredictable factors.

Even a clear fingerprint must be analyzed in the light of human behavior.

I had another interesting fingerprint case that further illustrates that even a fingerprint must sometimes be taken with a grain of salt.

A very wealthy bachelor had adopted and was raising two nephews. The boys were cousins, and the uncle was extraordinarily fond of them. It was generally understood that they were to inherit the uncle's great estate.

At the time of the incident I am relating, one of the boys was nineteen and the other was twenty-two.

The uncle kept some valuable securities, worth at least sixty thousand dollars, in a small manganese safe built into the living-room wall of his large house. One day when the uncle was out of town, the safe was robbed.

Hanging over the safe to conceal it was a mirror. On it were two very beautiful, very clear fingerprints; in fact they were so clear and so utterly convenient as to inspire caution. There were no marks anywhere else about the safe.

To the astonishment of the uncle, the fingerprints tallied exactly with those of the elder nephew. The old gentleman was heartbroken when I told him.

Wringing his hands, he repeated over and over, "Why did he do it? Why did he do it? He didn't have to do it. Why, that boy can have everything I've got. It is certainly strange; he's always been such a good boy. Do you think," he asked me, "that he really robbed the safe?"

I told him the truth—that I didn't know who robbed the safe. As for the young man, he nearly died of nervous prostration when the tests showed that the prints were his. He denied that he had robbed the safe. "And what's more," he declared, "I don't believe I ever touched that mirror in my life."

"Where were you at the time of the robbery?" I asked him.

His face lit up with sudden surprise and amazement. "Why," he said, "I remember now! I was out of town! I can prove it."

He did prove it to my complete satisfaction.

One rule I have always followed is never to take anything for granted. Consequently, I put everybody in the household under scrutiny. I studied the habits of the uncle and of the boys, got lists of their associates, checked every move they had made on the night of the robbery. Without telling anybody, I had operatives put on the trail of the boys.

One day the young woman whom I had employed to gain the confidence of the younger brother came in highly excited. She handed me a card on which was written an address.

"Get over there right away," she suggested, "and see what you can find."

The address was that of a rooming house. We found the room she had designated and learned it was rented by a young man who turned out to be the younger nephew. The room had been the scene of many a wild party, we learned, and some of the boy's associates were characters of notorious reputation.

We searched the boy's effects, and as suspected, among them was found an outfit for forging fingerprints! Thus the mystery of the fingerprints on the mirror was quickly solved. Their position on the mirror had also singled them out for special attention.

There are several methods of forging fingerprints, the most efficient being the inverse photo-engraving and swelled gelatine process. Perhaps, the less divulged about the method the better.

In this case the younger nephew was playing for big stakes. Not only did his greed and wild living crave the sixty thousand dollars, but he hoped to throw guilt to his cousin, thereby causing him to be disinherited. The crime had been carefully planned; a complete

fingerprint forging outfit rigged up. What the young man could
not foresee was his cousin's absence from the city on the night of
the crime. It is the unknowable element that proves tragic to the
crime career. In turn the plotter was disinherited.

Fortunately the forging of fingerprints is relatively rare. The
finger impression can usually be relied upon. Surprising as it may
seem, the criminal hardly ever wears gloves to prevent telltale
marks. He usually needs the free use of hands and fingers to feel
his way about a place. Gloves are a handicap. The intricate details
of blowing a safe preclude their use.

During the heightened tenseness of committing a crime the
criminal is more liable to leave a clear finger impression than at
any other time. Nervousness usually causes perspiration, and the
clammy wetness of the fingers is an ideal condition for a vivid
fingerprint.

If he has been in the clutches of the law previously, his doom is
virtually sealed if he leaves a finger mark. To the layman it may
seem a stupendous task to identify a finger impression among the
millions of prints on record. In the aggregate it is, but the finger-
printing system has become so thoroughly organized as to facili-
tate this work to a remarkable degree.

When a man is arrested for a crime, the local police take finger
impressions. This is done by spreading a thin coat of printer's ink
on a piece of glass or metal. Each of the subject's fingers is carefully rolled once on this ink-covered plate. The ink adheres to the
papillary ridges of the finger, and then it is likewise rolled on a
piece of blank paper, which prints the pattern in exactly the same
manner as a rubber stamp. Excellent finger impressions may be
made by placing the finger on a stamp pad and then placing them
on paper as a rubber stamp would be placed.

These fingerprints are then usually sent to the Federal Bureau
of Investigation, U. S. Department of Justice, Washington, D. C.
The recent figures reveal that over two million fingerprints of cur-
rent value are there filed for identification.

This filing has been simplified by the classification of fingerprint patterns into the following types: loops, twinned loops,

central pocket loops, lateral pocket loops, arches, tented arches, whorls, and accidentals.

By utilizing these patterns, together with the ridges intervening and surrounding two fixed points known as the core and the delta, a classification for the ten fingers has been developed. This classification permits the filing of fingerprint records in sequence without reference to name, description, or crime specialty of the individual, and enables the fingerprint expert in a bureau containing millions of prints to establish an identification in less than five minutes.

The Bureau at Washington receives an average of twelve hundred inquiries for fingerprint comparisons daily, and reports are returned within forty-eight hours.[1]

---

[1] "Criminal Identification," by J. Edgar Hoover, *Annals of the American Academy of Political and Social Science*, November, 1929.

4
A POCKETKNIFE AND A TWIG

A knife is found at the scene of a crime. Whose knife is it?

An ingeniously devised bomb is discovered. Who made it?

A burglar makes an entrance by means of certain tools. A suspect is arrested, and in his possession are found tools that might have been used for this purpose. Can the criminal investigator prove that these tools were so used?

From the days of Vidocq, who organized the first detective bureau in Paris at the beginning of the last century, until the present time, such questions have been answered largely by means of adducing circumstances, espionage, and reports of witnesses. In other words, the human element has played a major role in crime detection, and perhaps, always will.

Yet, how notoriously unreliable are the human factors! How many murderers have escaped the gallows because the authorities were unable to prove their guilt! How many innocent men have been imprisoned or hanged because people made mistakes either in identification or in reporting circumstances of the crimes committed!

No two eyewitnesses of a particular episode will make identical reports. What each sees is influenced by so many factors. A state of excitement or terror will distort the true picture. Memories are notoriously faulty. A small man dressed in white and seen in the dark will appear very tall. An ordinary object suddenly seen in the dark will appear immense. A medium-sized man dressed in a black suit will appear tall to the casual observer. If a strange object is seen for the first time, the observer will have no previous knowledge of its true nature, and hence optical illusions will lead him astray. Let an African savage view a railroad track for the first time and he will report that the rails meet in the distance. A house on a hill looks hardly large enough to accommodate a dog. Few people can accurately judge distances or dimensions. Many people fail to judge accurately from whence a sound comes, whether from below or from above; from the right or from the left. A wounded man or one immediately at the scene of the crime may be the most untrustworthy witness of all; for such persons often experience hallucinations, both visual and auditory.

Many witnesses lie without malice. Vanity may prompt some to fill in gaps in their story from pure imagination. Other witnesses may be moved by a mistaken zeal to be helpful to the investigator and report their own deductions and opinions as actual facts. Another may have an enemy whom he wishes to implicate, and the wish becomes the father of the report he gives—almost unconsciously sometimes.

From such flimsy threads the investigator must often weave the net that captures the criminal! Wonder it is that he succeeds as often as he does!

Obviously, the human element is far from perfect as a means of proof.

Science is fashioning supplementary tools from which the element of error has been eliminated almost entirely. Such means may lead directly to the criminal without the aid of witnesses, but more often they are a check on information that the investigator uncovers. Once the solution of a crime hinged on the ownership of a gun. A score of people claimed ownership of the weapon, but facts learned in the laboratory branded all these "positive" identifications as spurious. More of this anon in the chapter on guns and bullets.

One great advance in scientific criminal investigation has been made in the field of identification of knives, tools, and other instruments used by a criminal. Such identification has become a positive science.

For a great many years the writer has been actively engaged in the study of the identification of knives, tools, et cetera, for the purpose of determining with what degree of certainty they can be identified by microscopic marks left by their cutting edges or faces.

Exhaustive research has developed the fact that it is possible, under favorable circumstances, to identify the particular instrument, knife, or tool making a cut in metal, wood, or other stable substance.

It is gratifying to the writer that John H. Wigmore, dean emeritus of the Northwestern University faculty of law, saw fit to include in his work, *Principles of Judicial Proof*, the development of physical evidence as applied to the Clark case. This celebrated case is described later in this chapter.

All these findings are based upon the fact that when two metals or substances are pressed together with sufficient force, the softer metal or substance will conform to the surface irregularities of the harder metal.

The writer first became interested in making identifications of this sort in 1912 while seeking to identify the particular tool used in a screw-cutting lathe to cut fine threads on parts of a scientific instrument.

Microscopic examination of the cutting edges of the tools in question showed markings which were to characteristically different that it was quite obvious to anyone viewing them through the microscope which tool had cut the thread in question. These interesting results provoked further study. I was then engaged in designing and perfecting an instrument for the recording of sound to be used in detective work, and this work required a small but fully equipped machine shop.

It was not long before a series of experiments conclusively proved that practically every tool used in the shop could be positively identified. Lathe tools were ground with a very fine stone and then honed to a razorlike cutting edge, and even when so sharpened, the microscopic marks made by them in steel, brass, bronze, and copper could be identified as coming from the particular tool used.

Wood-working tools, chisels, turning tools, axes, etc., were then studied. An early application of the method was illustrated in the identification of a plane used to smooth the surface of a pine board forming the cover of a miniature casket in which an infant was buried. The identifying marks left by the imperfections in the bit of the plane in this instance were clearly visible when properly magnified.

Another early case in which this principle was used involved a mysterious burglary wherein thousands of dollars' worth of jewelry and clothing had been taken from a fashionable residence. The Yale lock on the front door had been badly battered by some heavy instrument. Experience told at a glance that entrance had not been effected by hammering the lock. Subsequent investigations showed that the marks had been made by a hammer in the hands of a maid-servant who, while the owners of the house were away, had packed the articles into a trunk of her own in the servants' quarter in the basement.

A laboratory examination of the lock showed the microscopic marks to fit identically similar microscopic imperfections on the face of a claw hammer found in the girl's room. This resulted in a confession and recovery of the goods, the lock having been damaged to create the impression that entrance had been gained by burglars from without.

Exhaustive research in hundreds of tests and examinations made of knife blades has proved to me that not only cuts made by a particular tool or instrument held in a fixed position, but also marks made by knives, tools, or other instruments held in the hand while cutting objects and moving from side to side or even twisting can be identified positively.

An interesting application of this principle was the identification of a knife used to sharpen a lead pencil which in turn was used to write a threatening letter. When the suspect was shown the photomicrograph of the pencil cuttings in comparison with those made by the knife found on his person, he made a complete confession.

The majority of such markings are invisible to the naked eye, many of them being less than one ten-thousandth of an inch in width and depth. Even ordinary commercial microscopes, comparison oculars, and devices for making accurate measurements applicable to ordinary laboratory work are often inadequate in many instances to this particular field of research. A number of special instruments for the simultaneous study and comparison of microscopic marks on two or more objects were, therefore, designed and constructed.

The scientific detective laboratory is not unlike that of a large industrial plant. There are samples of almost every known drug and chemical, several hundred samples of different kinds of substances ranging from writing inks to fabrics and fibres, hairs of all kinds of animals mounted on microscope plates, an enormous collection of every known type of bullet, delicately adjusted scales for weighing things no bigger than a speck of dust, calipers, test tubes, retorts, magnifying glasses.

For comparison of objects, the microscope is indispensable. So important is this aspect of laboratory work that I found it necessary to design what has been termed the Revelaroscope and mentioned in several scientific journals as one of the largest microscopes in the world. It is seven feet high and weighs more than half a ton. It has magnification range of from two to five thousand diameters. Instead of looking through a small glass at the object under scrutiny, you see it spread before you on a field ten inches in diameter. The object, viewed through a series of lens complements, becomes a very plain picture on a translucent screen; and a hair viewed through this instrument appears like a telegraph pole. Two pieces of paper may seem identical to the naked eye; but under the microscope any difference in texture may be seen as plainly as the difference between burlap and chiffon.

Another instrument, known as the Magnascope, enables the observer to view, greatly magnified, as many as four different objects in apposition or juxtaposition, as in the comparison of bullets. It also permits the fusion of all images or one with another by superimposition. It has proved invaluable in examining typewriting, printing, seals, etchings, marks, etc.

The application of these instruments in crime detection may be illustrated in a rape and murder case I have in mind. What looked like a speck of dust was found in the genitalia of the murdered girl. A minute bit of fir needle was found on the generative organs of the suspected man. The photomicrograph proved conclusively that the speck of dirt was the tip of the fir needle, and this evidence convinced the jury of eight men and four women; the convicted man was executed for this brutal crime.

More significant is the Clark case, in which the Supreme Court of the State of Washington established a precedent relevant to the admissibility in a court of law of physical evidence secured in a laboratory by purely scientific instruments and methods. It is to be expected that the courts are cautious in accepting new ideas and new methods, for even the so-called expert is subject to error. The outstanding progressive decision in the Clark case is a significant step forward.

Read the decision:

Courts are no longer skeptical that by the aid of scientific appliances, the identity of a person may be established by fingerprints. There is no difference in principle in the utilization of the photomicrograph to determine that the same tool that made one impression is the same instrument that made another impression. The edge on one blade differs as greatly from the edge on another blade as do the lines on one human hand differ from the lines on another. This is a progressive age. The scientific means afforded should be used to apprehend the Criminal.

This now famous precedent was made on December 28, 1930. The crime that concerned the court was committed on December 6, 1928.

A happy little girl left the school at Roy, Washington, to saunter homeward through a wooded lane. With Christmas only a few days away she was probably day-dreaming of Santa Claus, when a man leaped out from behind a clump of bushes near the roadside. Ruthlessly he threw a cloth over the girl's head, dragged her into the thicket, and there brutally assaulted her.

When released she was forced to leave without looking back, thereby hiding the identity of her assailant.

Sheriff Tom Desmond, of Tacoma, Washington, hurried to the scene of the crime. Questioning the girl did very little good, for she had only a vague idea of her assailant's size and stature.

"That description might fit any of us," he remarked to his deputy.

On three successive occasions the authorities made an intensive search of the scene of the crime, but so clever had the assailant been in covering up his tracks, that nothing was found. In making this search, one of the officers grabbed a young sapling to move it out of his way. Lo and behold it came out of the ground with very little effort. Seven such saplings were found.

The depraved creature who had committed the crime had carefully built a blind or screen of fir boughs to conceal himself from view. He had cut a number of boughs and saplings, placed them near a fir tree alongside the trail, thus cleverly simulating the surrounding growth.

Several small branches about one-half inch in diameter had been cut with a knife. The cut ends were sticking in the ground under the lower branches of the tree. Behind this screen the brute was concealed as he lay in wait for his victim.

"This doesn't offer us much of a clue," Sheriff Desmond commented. "A few things are obvious. The man was not a transient stranger. He knew of the girl and of the trail she followed home from school. He is known in the community and perhaps by the girl; otherwise he would not have been so careful to conceal himself behind a mask. He is probably a sex-starved bachelor, whose isolated life has perverted both his mind and body."

Sheriff Desmond then began a seemingly fruitless search for such a character. The community at Roy is small, and hence everyone in it is more or less known. Nine men were selected as possible suspects. Careful investigation eliminated all but one—a man by the name of Clark who lived alone in a hotel at Roy.

In the meantime Sheriff Desmond had shown exceedingly good judgment in preserving all the cut branches found at the scene of the crime. "Of what possible use can they be?" a deputy asked with a skeptical smile.

"Frankly, I haven't the least idea," Desmond replied, "but it's the rule of the game to pick up everything at the scene of a crime that isn't locked, screwed, or bolted."

Clark's room at the hotel was entered by the sheriff and his deputy. They had not the slightest evidence against the man other than that he was a suspicious character about town who might be guilty. Extralegal means are often justifiable. They proved so in this case.

Clark was seated on the bed when the officers entered. He gave a start, which Desmond's shrewd, sharp eyes noted. His shifty dark eyes roved about the room in an endless parade of confusion. Otherwise the man seemed calm and collected.

Desmond was sure of his man.

"Did you cut those cedar branches?" Desmond pointed to a couple of boughs that had been hung on the wall as Christmas decorations.

"Yes," Clark growled sulkily. "What of it?" Desmond decided to play a bold hand.

"You are under arrest for the assault of ——."

The man loudly protested his innocence. He was searched. Among other things taken from his person was a three-bladed pocketknife.

"Did you cut those cedar limbs with this knife?" The man admitted that he had.

The sheriff then sent to my laboratory the following items:

The fir boughs found at the scene of the crime.

The three-bladed pocketknife taken from the defendant.

The two cedar boughs taken from the defendant's room.

To the layman these slight bits of evidence seem ridiculously inadequate, and with only the naked eye to view them they would be.

However, the knife was examined, and on the large blade was found pitch such as comes from fir trees. Under the microscope the blade showed the usual microscopic irregularities in the cutting edge of a knife that has been used and carefully sharpened. None of the other blades showed signs of pitch.

An instrument was designed by the writer resembling the human arm including shoulder, elbow, and wrist joints, with variable adjustments simulating the shoulder and elbow movements. The part holding the knife has adjustments which can be controlled and varied by a series of cams, pawls, and levers, allowing the holder to simulate the degree of circumduction supination, and pronation of the wrist in the act of making a given cut.

With this device it is possible to duplicate repeatedly the same cut, using the same portion of the blade each time, the blade entering and passing through the wood at the same angle with relation to the plane surface of the portion cut.

A number of cuts were made in fir boughs and saplings of the same size taken from the same trees from which the boughs were cut at the scene of the crime. These cuttings were then compared under the comparison magnascope until the angle at which the knife was held was determined. A perfect match resulted from cuts made with the knife held as in the right hand.

Photomicrographs were made of the cuts, and identifying marks enumerated. None of these marks were discernible until highly magnified.

Considering only the major marks on this cut, it can be mathematically determined that no other blade in the world would make a cut like this. Under the law of probabilities, by the algebraic formula for determining combinations and permutations, with only one-third of the marks shown as factors, there would be only one chance of there being another blade exactly like this if every one of the hundred million people in the United States had six hundred and fifty quadrillion knives each. Using all the marks and the factors of depth, width, shape, etc., it would carry to infinity.

Clark was tried before Judge Hodge of the Superior Court of Pierce County, Washington. The cut branches that were used in the construction of the blind, the stumps from which they were cut, together with large photomicrographs of the surface of the cuts, were offered in evidence.

The jury convicted Clark, and Judge Hodge gave him a sentence of twenty to thirty years in the penitentiary. He appealed, but the Supreme Court in the decision already cited upheld Judge Hodge and established a precedent which has already been cited in criminal trials in many other states, thereby legally advancing science in its battle against crime.

5
WHEN GUNS TALK

Pseudo-experts in ballistic jurisprudence, fingerprinting, and allied criminological subjects are springing up by the hundreds whose purpose may be above reproach; but scientific crime detection cannot be accomplished by the mere use of a textbook and microscope. Not only do such so-called "experts" bring disrepute on scientific crime detection in criminal courts, but they are a real menace to the administration of justice. Years of exhaustive study and special experience are necessary to qualify as an expert on firearms in this special field. A case comes to mind.

A woman was facing trial for murder, her life hanging in the balance and the noose staring her in the face. Conviction depended on finding the gun that had fired the fatal bullet. A man had been shot, and the woman was accused of the crime. A .38 calibre lead bullet was the only clue, for the gun was not located by the police.

The bullet found in the dead man's body would seem to the layman like any other bullet of the same calibre. A so-called firearm expert declared the bullet was from a .38 rim-fire. This opinion was interesting to the sheriff, for that type of firearm was scarce, and this fact would narrow the search to a limited field. He delegated a deputy sheriff to make the search for a .38 rim-fire pistol or revolver among people directly or indirectly connected with the crime.

The deputy picked up the bullet, and with hardly a glance at it, casually remarked: "Why, this is a bullet made by the United States Cartridge Company, loaded in their .38 short Colt ammunition."

48

He claimed to have taken a thirty-days' course in firearm identification and forensic ballistics. Admirable as his ambition was, his snap judgment and lack of knowledge were deplorable.

The sheriff scratched his head in bewilderment. Here were two so-called experts who gave divergent opinions. Both were willing to swear by their opinions though a woman's life depended on their testimony. Shrewder than most, the sheriff demanded proof from his two experts. None was forthcoming, and after a conference with the prosecuting attorney, the sheriff jumped into his automobile and brought the bullet in question and some blood- and powder-stained clothing to the laboratory.

The bullet was weighed; its shape and groove data looked up in the index of files containing thousands of specimen bullets and shells. In the files the exact duplicate of the fired bullet was found. It was not loaded in the United States Cartridge Company's .38 short Colt; neither was it from a rim-fire. It was of foreign manufacture.

The rifling marks on the bullet also showed it to have been fired from a revolver of foreign manufacture when compared with shop data and specimens of a certain manufacturer of cheap revolvers. Powder marks on the clothing showed them to be from a certain make of powder not in use in this country.

A search of the shipping records of the American importer of these revolvers revealed the name of a man located in the town where the murder was committed, to whom such a gun and ammunition had been sent. He was found with the gun in his possession, and further laboratory tests showed conclusively that the bullet found in the dead man's body had been fired by this particular revolver. The woman suspect was released, and the owner of the gun convicted.

We cite this case merely to illustrate the fact that firearm identification and forensic ballistics is an exact science that demands much knowledge, experience, and laboratory equipment.

1. Which *one* of *six* identical revolvers fired the fatal shot?
2. Is it *suicide, murder,* or *accident?*

3. Was the shooting in *self-defense?*
4. Was the *bullet* fired in this particular *gun?*
5. Did this *bullet* strike anything *before* hitting the *victim?*
6. What make, type, and calibre of gun did this shooting?
7. Was this empty *shell* fired in this particular *gun?*
8. Were there *more* than two *guns* used?
9. What type, make, calibre, *rifle* or *revolver* fired this *shell?*
10. (Without bullet or shell) Could this gun have caused the wound?
11. Through what substance did this bullet pass?
12. Which one of seven bullets passed through a human body?
13. Could the wound have been self-inflicted?
14. Which of *three* different *bullets*, all passing through body, caused death, and which particular *gun* fired it?

About twenty years ago the writer, an ardent rifle and pistol shooter, began this particular study, including the collection of cartridges, bullets, and powders of every known make. It was—and is—a never-ending task. Those so collected were added to the collection of the Institute of Scientific Criminology, which contains samples secured from every manufacturer, shells, bullets, cartridges, powder, and primers. Thousands of cartridges have been filed and indexed.

There are probably fewer than half a dozen such collections in the United States for the exclusive purpose of criminological research.

Identification of ammunition is only one of the many important phases of forensic ballistics. Is it possible to demonstrate with scientific accuracy the difference between a bullet hitting a bone in a human body, and a bullet ricochetted from objects before entering the body? The expert can prove a vital difference. A Seattle policeman was acquitted of murder by such evidence. It was proved that the bullet fired from his gun had ricochetted and did not hit the innocent person direct.

Identifying a gun by the bullet it fires is, perhaps, the most common problem that the investigator is asked to solve. Also it is the most common route to the gallows. Not long ago there occurred a typical case.

Two bandits held up a number of automobiles on a highway. Deputy sheriffs got on their trail, and when they found them, a running gun fight took place. When the smoke of battle cleared, a deputy sheriff was found dead. The two gunmen escaped in an automobile.

A short time later this motor car, previously stolen by the bandits, was found, and in it was one of the bandits—dead. Alongside him was a gun with most of the shells discharged.

It had been thought that the bandit who escaped was the one who had killed the deputy sheriff, but a microscopic examination of the fatal bullets showed that they had come from the very gun the dead bandit held in his hand. These bullets had the same peculiar characteristic markings—such as are made by the rifling of the barrel—as those shown by test bullets fired from the gun.

But the biggest surprise of all came when, in the laboratory, I examined the bullet that had killed the bandit, and found that it had come from the gun found alongside his body. By the time the gun was submitted to me it had been handled by more than thirty persons. There wasn't an intelligible fingerprint on it—just a jumble.

The escaped bandit was trailed down and taken into custody; in the course of his examination by the officers, he was shown the gun which had been found in the car with his pal.

"Was this your gun?" he was asked.

"I never saw that gun before in my life," he answered. With this statement he overstepped himself and made a fatal mistake.

For several days we studied the gun, for we wanted to make sure whether or not the bandit was telling the truth. It had what gunmen call a "sweet action," a smooth pull of the trigger. Acting on a hunch, I disassembled the gun. In a few moments I knew that the arrested man had lied to us. His fingerprints were plainly visible on the inner workings of the gun, placed there at the time he had "doctored" the weapon.

When he was confronted with this evidence, the characteristic fear of the criminal prompted him to confess. He had killed not only the deputy sheriff, but his pal as well—the deputy to avoid arrest, and his pal, on the theory that dead men tell no tales.

Another recent case of how guns talk and bring vengeance on the heads of murderers is that of the killing of John Joseph Wright, British war hero who won three medals during the World War.

After the war Wright had emigrated to America and on September 20, 1930, found himself in Shelby, Montana, the little oil and cow town made famous by the Dempsey-Gibbons world championship fight. Shortly after midnight he boarded a through freight train roaring toward Great Falls. Soon he was sound asleep.

At the same time three other man boarded a car on the train, "beating their way" to Great Falls. As they sat there in the darkness chatting about inconsequential things, two dark figures appeared over the swaying crest of a tank car and jumped down beside them.

"Stick 'em up!" The fear-inspiring command came like a bolt from a dark sky. In the flicker of a flashlight the men saw the glint of a gun. Two of the freight train passengers were penniless, but the other had $50 which was quickly removed by one of the robbers.

"Jump for it, you fellows!" A warning shot quickly enforced this second command.

The men jumped, but one of them, C. C. Dorris, an ex-railroader, sprinted alongside the train and soon swung himself aboard one of the tail-end cars.

Dorris had met Wright at Shelby and had taken a liking to this wandering war hero who was trying to carve a career for himself in the new world. He had seen Wright swing aboard the train alone, and now wondered if the robbers had also run into him.

Cautiously Dorris crept forward along the line of cars until he came to the lumber gondola that Wright had boarded. He found the ex-soldier slumped over where he sat. Pulling his coat, he called to him. No response. The man was dead. Dorris hurriedly notified the conductor.

The train rolled into Great Falls, Montana, when day was breaking, and there was met by Bob Gordon, sheriff of Cascade County, and Frank P. Gault, prosecuting attorney. They found that Wright had been shot through the heart. Beside him were his war medals and passport, where the bandits had contemptuously cast them aside. Also there were three empty shells from an automatic .32 calibre revolver. In the car where Dorris and his two companions had been held up was found another similar shell—the warning shot fired when the men had jumped.

Dorris remembered two suspicious-looking characters he had seen at Shelby, and whom he suspected of the crime, though in the darkness of the night he could not be sure. However, he gave a good description of these two men, and soon radio station KFBB was sending out descriptions of the pair over the air.

The two men, Thomas Harrison Groves, alias Bert Williams, and Harry E. Miller, had left the train at Conrad, Montana, and were heading toward Fort Benton when they were trapped. They begged a meal and a night's lodging from a farm woman. She had heard the description of the men over her radio and immediately notified the sheriff at Conrad.

The men were soon captured, but denied ever having been at Shelby. Groves, however, had a .32 calibre Spanish automatic pistol and a box nearly full of Peters cartridges for the weapon. This fact was significant, for the shells found at the scene of the crime were also Peters cartridges.

Now came the question of jurisdiction. What county would conduct the prosecution? As the murder had been committed on a moving train, it was impossible to know in which county Wright had been killed. The case finally went to trial at Conrad, Montana, with E. E. Sweitzer, prosecuting attorney of Pondera County, Walter R. Knaack, county attorney of Toole County, Bert Packer, county attorney of Teton County, and Art Jardine, chief criminal deputy prosecutor of Great Falls, participating in the prosecuting. A situation, no doubt, unique in criminal procedure in this country.

It was science, represented by the radio, that led to the capture, and it was science that brought about conviction.

Though the two men were positively identified as having been in Shelby on the night of the murder, there was no way of identifying them as the men who had committed the crime on the freight train.

However, the pistol and shells had been sent to the laboratory. There the shells and gun were examined. Test shots were fired, using the loaded cartridges found on Groves at the time of his arrest.

At the trial I produced greatly enlarged photomicrographs of the bases of the four shells found at the scene of the crime and of the test-shells fired in the laboratory, together with a photomicrograph of the breechblock of the confiscated pistol.

Under the giant comparison magnascope, the breechblock showed ridges and hollows (invisible to the naked eye) made by the file of the mechanic who had finished the weapon at the factory. Each time the gun was fired, the base of the cartridge shell had been pressed against this breechblock under thousands of pounds' pressure, and the breechblock had left its imprint on the soft metal of the cartridge primer in the same manner that a steel die stamps a pattern on softer material.

Although invisible to the naked eyes, there were over twenty major points on the breechblock showing distinguishing characteristics—peculiar patterns left by the mechanic's tools. And in every instance the shells—four found at the scene of the crime and those fired in the laboratory—were plainly marked and embossed with the identical microscopic pattern from the breechblock.

These large photomicrographs were presented in court. The jury soon became convinced that the shells all had the same characteristic markings, and a comparison with the pits and ridges of the breechblock was sufficient to convince them that the shells had been fired from the same gun. And it was Groves' gun!

Groves and Miller both drew sentences of life imprisonment, fixed in each instance by the jury in its verdict. It was probably one of the oddest trials in the history of Montana. Never before had four counties united in prosecuting one trial.

So conclusive was the "demonstrable evidence" identifying the deadly weapon that the defense counsel, in argument, implied that the officers had sent shells to the laboratory which they had themselves fired in Groves' gun. This course, however, was adopted after an unsuccessful attempt to discredit the identification through ineffective cross-examination.

6
WHEN GUNS TALK (CONTINUED)

A brush fire on a vacant lot in the city of Tacoma, Washington, attracted the usual coterie of small boys making sport with the flames. Suddenly there were heard three distinct explosions in the burning brush. Curiosity is the heritage of boys, and hence the youngsters proceeded to investigate the source of the explosions as soon as the fire had subsided. There they found an automatic pistol, old, rusty, and apparently worthless.

This episode seemed an insignificant thing, but behind it lay a tragedy that had been a mystery to authorities for four long years. It is just such cases as the Hallen murder mystery that give color to the thought that there is a stalking Nemesis that brings doom, sooner or later, to the enemies of society.

Not only was the finding of the gun that killed Harry Hallen an odd play of Fate, but the seemingly miraculous preservation of the breechblock—one of the vital parts of a gun that will "talk" to the criminologist—was almost uncanny.

On the night of March 11, 1921, Harry Hallen, World War veteran and superintendent of the Criffen Wheel Works, Tacoma, was walking home in company with his wife. They had attended a party at the home of Mrs. Hallen's parents, and there seemed to be nothing at hand to mar the happiness or the promising future of this young and talented couple.

Suddenly shots rang out in the dark night, and Hallen fell to the ground the victim of an unknown assailant.

Two empty shells of .45 calibre found at the scene of the crime were the only clue. However, it was significant that only a short time previously a similar but unsuccessful attack had been made upon Nick Cramer, another official of the wheel works. This fact fathered the theory that, perhaps, a disgruntled workman had suddenly turned assassin.

Investigation showed that a man, whom we will call Sponi Gadino, had been discharged from the factory a short time previously, and that Hallen had been instrumental in the dismissal. But Gadino could not be found for questioning, and his fellow countrymen refused to talk, as is usually the case with this type of Italian. No doubt their silence is motivated by a fear of revenge. Furthermore, there was not an iota of evidence against him, though authorities made a nation-wide search to find him.

Empty cartridges found at the scene of the attack on Cramer gave further indication that the assault was made by a Griffen plant worker with a grudge. A laboratory examination of the shells found at the scene of the Hallen murder and those at the scene of the Cramer attack showed them to have been fired from the same gun. Viewed under the microscope, these shells showed distinctive identifying marks on the base caused by the breechblock, the firing-pin different from any other .45 automatic pistol. Both sets of shells were obviously fired from the same gun, but they in themselves would not constitute a means of identifying the particular gun firing them. That could be done only through finding the assailant's weapon.

Over a period of three years many guns were submitted to me for examination, but none of them proved to be the gun that killed Hallen. It seemed that the Hallen murder would forever be a mystery until four years later when a group of boys found a rusty old automatic .45 in the burning brush three blocks from the Hallen home.

In the meantime Gadino remained under suspicion. This was strengthened when two years after the crime an acquaintance of the man reported that Gadino had fled the country when he learned that "Tacoma Police were after him." A police tip from Chicago led a Tacoma detective to that city, but the search seemed futile. The four-year search finally ended in San Francisco, where an insurance company had Gadino arrested on an arson charge. From police records it was learned that he was wanted in Tacoma. In San Francisco the accused had fallen in love with a young lady; but when she married another man, he reverted to his old phobia of revenge and set fire to the home of the girl's father. When searching Gadino's room to verify suspicions, San Francisco authorities found a veritable arsenal of weapons and explosives.

In the meantime Tacoma police officials sent the rusty pistol picked up by the boys to the laboratory. It seemed a hopeless gesture to secure evidence against Gadino. Fingerprints, of course, were rusted away beyond any recognition, both externally and internally.

However, after seven days of careful treatment with oil and gentle forcing, the gun was reconditioned to the extent that it could be fired. On removing the magazine, two exploded shells and bullets were found, evidently having been fired from ignition by external heat. No doubt, these were the two shells exploded in the brush fire, and that prompted the boys to make a search of the premises. In the chamber of the pistol was found a fired shell.

Most remarkable was the condition of the breechblock. It was in excellent state of preservation—one of those freak situations that are often unexplainable, and that just as often bring a murderer to the gallows. This gun was in condition to "talk," after lying in the rain and muck for four years! A thin film of oil, having been protected by the base of the shell in immediate contact with the breechblock, preserved this part better than any other part of the pistol.

Using a special camera for photographing breechblocks through the barrel of the pistol, we produced a photomicrograph, magnified hundreds of times, which showed fine machine marks clearly defined across the entire face of the breechblock and around the firing-pin hole. There were five such major marks which do not appear on the breechblocks of other automatic pistols, because they were defects and marks impressed into the face of the breechblock by a soldier who indented the breechblock with a ramrod while cleaning it.

When the explosion takes place in the Colt's .45 automatic pistol, the sleeve, surrounding the barrel which is also integral with the breechblock, is forced backwards, and the extractor on the right-hand side of the breechblock pulls the fired shell back out of the chamber in its rearward motion.

The ejector protrudes through the breechblock, forcing the shell outward and upward, so that the mechanism of the pistol is cleared. The mark left by this ejector is used as a starting point to locate other marks on the base of the shell as the ejector mark will be found in the same relative position to other identifying marks on all shells fired in the same pistol.

These examinations and photographs showed conclusively that the shells found at the scene of the Hallen murder and those at the Cramer assault had been fired from this particular gun found rusty and decrepit in the burning brush! The gun told us that much, but could not tell its former owner.

Tacoma detectives then began the arduous task of finding the owner. They learned that this particular gun had been stolen from a military reservation near the city, and they finally traced the gun to Sponi Gadino. That was the last link in the chain of evidence.

This Colt's automatic told its story; its owner was found, convicted, and sentenced to life imprisonment. The uncanny story told by the gun at the trial cast a spell of awe over the spectators. Truly "the way of the transgressor is hard."

Sponi Gadino appealed his case on a technical rule relative to the admissibility of some evidence, and the high court sent the case back for retrial. In the meantime, however, witnesses had left the state; therefore the prosecutor, rather than retry the case, surrendered the prisoner to the California authorities to be tried for arson.

7
BODY WOUNDS — WHAT THEY TELL

In the classroom of the School of Scientific Police at the Palais de Justice in Paris is a truism: "The eyes see in things only what they look for, and they look only for what is already in the mind."

This might well be a universal warning in crime detection, for often the most significant bit of evidence is overlooked or misinterpreted because some one has jumped to a premature conclusion. The detective who quickly reconstructs a crime without sufficient supporting evidence is very liable to spend days, weeks, and perhaps months on a wrong scent in a vain effort to make evidence fit his personal version of what happened at the scene of the crime. He looks only for what is already in his mind. Unconsciously, perhaps, he may try to convict an innocent victim who he believes committed a crime while the real perpetrator takes advantage of the wild-goose chase to make a clean get-away.

To face a crime with an open mind—a mind willing to believe and disbelieve even its own senses, sometimes willing to admit and desert one line of investigation for another, is one of the most difficult tasks of the detective. He is human, and like all other humans he is subject to personal prejudice.

Violent death may appear to be murder, or it may appear to be a clear case of suicide. The well-trained detective doesn't make a snap judgment. He weighs the physical evidence very carefully, and often this evidence is only the body of the deceased. Body marks tell the story. Sometimes the condition of a body may seem to mislead or tell conflicting stories.

59

60

Luke S. May

In practically every morgue in the country there are bodies of unknown persons found from time to time that resist ordinary efforts of determining cause of death. Many such find their way to the pauper's grave, and their secrets are buried with them. The degree of success in solving such cases varies with the skill and facilities available to the coroner.

Usually such cases call for experts in medical and allied sciences. The general practitioner of medicine cannot be expected to be an expert in medicolegal science or forensic medicine. Even the skilled pathologist must often seek aid from the immunologist, the chemist, the toxicologist, and the bacteriologist.

This contention is freely admitted by the well known doctor, George Burgess Magrath, A.M., M.D., professor in legal medicine, Harvard University, medical examiner for Suffolk County, Massachusetts:

Fifty years ago any physician was considered competent to make a satisfactory post-mortem examination. Today such examinations are generally regarded as matters properly for the pathologist, whose services must be sought if the cause of death is to be discovered with scientific accuracy. The last half century has witnessed the changes and advances in medicine which have made specialization inevitable and rendered individual proficiency in every branch impossible, and the general practitioner of today, whenever in need of knowledge or skill beyond his own, unhesitatingly calls to his aid a specialist.[1]

Further, the medicolegal expert must have, besides a medical technique, a skill and experience in crime methods more or less commensurate with that of the detective. That is, he must often visit the scene of the crime in order to reconstruct, if possible, what

[1] "Medical Science in the Service of the State," by George Burgess Magrath, A.M., M.D., *Annals of the American Academy of Political and Social Science*, November, 1929.

actually happened to cause the death in question. His power of deduction must be well developed. Fingernail marks on the front of the neck of the deceased may seem insignificant to the layman, but considered in the light of internal damage disclosed in the post-mortem examination, they may establish the fact that the victim came to his death by manual strangulation.

A man was shot and a cursory examination revealed four bullet wounds in the man's abdomen and thigh, each wound discolored (black and blue marks or ecchymoses). The doctor making the examination declared the man to have been shot four times from the front at close range, the discolorations being attributed to powder burns. This supported the statement of a witness that the man had been shot in cold blood while his hands were raised. Further investigation of the wounds in a more thorough manner, and by means of reconstructing the crime as it actually happened, revealed that the man had been shot only twice. One shot had hit him from the side as he stooped over, and his decided paunch, the layers of flesh forming ridges, made it possible for one bullet to penetrate one of these ridges and then enter the thigh. Thus one bullet made three definite holes in the front of the man's body. This finding discredited the witness and opened a new angle of investigation, which revealed that the murdered man himself had participated in the shooting fray. These body wounds, though at first misinterpreted, were directly responsible for the solution of the crime.

Then there was the case of a murder in which the defendant pleaded self-defense. However, his story of the quarrel seemed rather thin. Again the body told the true story. A superficial examination was made by an untrained medic. No wounds. However, we performed a thorough autopsy; shaving the head, we first found at the top of the murdered man's skull a slight indentation, into which the butt of the defendant's gun fitted exactly, and further examination disclosed he had been struck several times. Obviously the murdered man had been attacked with the butt of the gun after being shot, a fact which indicated that the defendant had been in a state of furious anger at the time of the killing. Legally, this additional attack with the butt of the gun precluded the plea of self-defense.

A characteristic case of misinterpreting body marks was that of the mystifying death of George S. Simmons. Officers discovered a plausible motive for murder, and contributing circumstances wove a web of incriminating evidence around the suspect that seemed a sure trap. I will tell the story as it unfolded itself to the authorities at the time. It was known as the "Mystery of Cushman Dam."

On a bright clear morning of November 23, 1930, the body of "Curly" Simmons was found slumped in the seat of his car. Even a casual glance indicated that the handsome, twenty-three-year-old man was dead. The face that usually wore a happy smile was drawn in lines of agony, and his mop of curly brown hair that made him a striking figure to feminine admirers was in disarray. In the front of his overcoat was a large jagged tear, blood-stained. On his knees lay a high-powered Springfield army rifle.

Such was the report brought back to authorities by a man whom we will call Harry Matthews, a close friend of Simmons, who had found the body in an automobile near the Cushman Dam, Shelton, Washington.

Both Matthews and Simmons were employed by the City of Tacoma at its electric power project at Lake Cushman. On the forest-covered shore of this placid lake are a group of picturesque cottages and a few more pretentious homes that a stranger would assume to be a colony of city folk enjoying life in the wilderness for the summer. It is, however, a year-around colony of people employed by the City of Tacoma at its hydroelectric development on Lake Cushman.

The tragic death of Simmons, a member of this colony, was a striking contrast to the idyllic life of these people in the quiet and peace of virgin lake and forest. The little community at "Camp A" was stunned, for "Curly" Simmons was one of the most popular of the younger set, an unmarried young man who was the life of every party. No one knew he had an enemy or a care in the world.

Tracing back, the local officials learned that Simmons had attended a lodge meeting and dance at Union City the evening before his death. From there he and a companion had gone to a friend's home where a party was in progress. There he found Mr. and Mrs. Matthews, his best friends. It was reported that he had danced several numbers with Mrs. Matthews. He had seemed gay and carefree. After the tragedy some members of the community hinted that Simmons had been entirely too friendly with the pretty young wife of his friend and fellow worker. Rumor had it that perhaps this was a love triangle with jealousy as a motive. Subsequent developments pointed in that direction.

Two physicians were called to view the body. They found a small hole in the victim's back, and a much larger gash in his chest. The clothing near the chest wound had apparently been blown outward by the force of the bullet's exit, and the doctors immediately gave the opinion that Simmons had been shot in the back from some distance away with a high-powered rifle using a soft-nose bullet. A bullet hole was also found in one of the car doors.

It seemed a clear case of murder to the investigators. It is human nature to expect the worst in the case of a violent death, and usually such suppositions are correct.

Now to find the assailant. The rumors that Harry Matthews had reason to be jealous of Simmons, along with the fact that it was Matthews who had found the body on that early Sunday morning, made him the chief subject of investigation.

He was arrested, and a gun and soft-nosed bullets found at his home.

"Do you own a Winchester 1895 model 30 Government army rifle?" Officers put this question to Matthews.

"Yes." The suspect seemed sullen and morose.

"What type of bullet do you use?"

"Soft-nosed."

This reply elicited a gleam of elation in the inquisitor's eyes. There is always the intense excitement of the chase in the manhunt. Also it is remarkable how incriminating facts pile up when a man is arrested for a crime and a motive is discovered. The most trifling event seems significant.

"You carried this gun on the morning that Simmons was murdered?"

"Yes."

"And you fired the shot that killed Simmons?" The officer's staccato voice barked the question.

Matthews' face turned a deep crimson. "No! I hadn't fired the gun for three weeks before that time."

"How come you were near the scene of the crime at the time it occurred?"

"Simmons and I were going out deer-hunting, but he didn't show up; so I went out alone."

"Do you know that it is rumored that Simmons was very attentive to your wife?"

Something very near a sob choked the suspect. "It's a lie! He was my best friend!"

The questioning brought no results except to tighten the net of suspicion about Matthews.

Two doctors had given the positive opinion that Simmons had been shot from the rear at considerable distance with a rifle using a soft-nosed bullet. Matthews had been near the scene of the crime with such a gun and bullets at about the time Simmons was killed. It looked bad for Matthews, to say the least. Simmons' rifle was loaded with hard-nosed bullets.

A further search of the scene of the crime revealed a note:

I will pay for it if Belt don't.
Curly.

Some declared this note was a forgery to give color to the suicide theory—financial worry or some sort of trouble. Captain Strickland, chief of detectives of the City of Tacoma, had been called into the case, and he submitted the note and several specimens of handwriting to me and asked that I go over the scene of the shooting with him.

When we went out to the scene of the crime, we made a very careful investigation of all phases, trying to dismiss from our minds everything that had been related to us about the case, including the opinions of the two physicians.

We first examined the bullet hole in the door of Simmons' automobile. It was obvious that the bullet had passed from the inside of the car to the outside, the bullet hole in the upholstering being identical in size and shape with the holes in the shirt, the underwear, the sweater, and overcoat worn by Simmons. The shape of these holes indicated that the bullet had "keyholed"; that is, it had turned in its flight to an end-over-end movement instead of nose forward, the natural position of a bullet in flight. It was evident that the axis of the oval hole was identical in the victim's clothing and in the material of the car door.

We removed the upholstering and took specimens of the padding for laboratory tests. Further we cleaned the inside of the hole where the bullet had passed through the metal part of the door, this substance also being preserved for laboratory tests. These tests showed traces of human blood, showing that the bullet that punctured the door had previously passed through a human body. This exploded a previous theory advanced that the hole in the car door had been caused by a shot other than the one that caused the death of Simmons. The shape of the hole in the car further established the fact that the bullet that had passed through Simmons' body was also the bullet that had penetrated the door of his automobile.

The exact shape and size of the bullet hole in the car door and that in the man's clothing at the back indicated that the hole in Simmons' back was the hole of exit. In other words Simmons had been shot from the front, contrary to the opinions of physicians. A new theory of the crime must be formulated.

And still the large gash in the chest of the victim, the frayed edges of the clothing, apparently blown outward as the bullet emerged mushroomed, had to be satisfactorily explained. The apparent absence of powder burns on the clothing would seem to indicate a shot fired from a distance, in accord with the doctors' opinion. It all seemed very confusing.

In the laboratory I constructed a dummy, simulating the nature of human flesh, and covered it with the victim's clothing. Then taking Simmons' Springfield rifle and one of his full metal-jacketed bullets I fired into the dummy, holding the muzzle in direct contact with the clothing.

The bullet made a hole identical with that found in the front of the clothing Simmons wore. It was a large crisscross tear with the frayed edges pointing outward. The hole in the back of the dummy was small.

This is what happened: The gas blast of the gun continues on with the bullet into the hole in the body, thereby causing a terrible laceration when the gas seeks to escape. In fact the hole in the body becomes a continuation of the gun barrel, and in this gun, which has a breech pressure of upwards of forty thousand pounds per square inch, the force of the explosion, or rather the gas blast expanding in the hole made by the bullet caused more destruction to tissue than the bullet itself. To the inexperienced eye this type of body wound might easily be confused with the wound of exit caused by a soft-nosed bullet.

This tremendous breech pressure and expanding gas being released within the hole made by the bullet of a gun held close to the body was responsible for the great tearing force which in turn was blown back toward the muzzle of the gun, much in the same manner as a stream of water under high pressure in a nozzle directed against a wall will spatter water directly back against the nozzle.

In this case the wound of entrance had the appearance of being blown out, a shredded appearance with the shreds of clothing and flesh coming outward.

The absence of definite powder burns is easily explained. Very few, if any, powder marks will be observed upon clothing of a dark color in the event the muzzle of a .30 '06 Springfield rifle is held in immediate contact with an object when it is discharged, for barrel residue and unburned grains of powder along with the expanding gas can form no immediate cone of dispersion but usually follow the path of the bullet into the body. However, in this case one unburned grain of powder was found on the inner lining of the front of the overcoat, proving conclusively that the shot had been fired from the front and that the bullet had entered the chest.

Who fired the bullet?

After these laboratory findings Captain Strickland and I returned to the scene of the crime. With the facts we had learned we tried to reenact the scene of death. For this purpose we used a detective of the same size and general build as Simmons.

The detective got into Simmons' car. A deputy sheriff described as nearly as possible how Simmons had slumped over the wheel of his car when the death bullet had struck him. The Springfield rifle was placed in the position in which it was found, as nearly as the local officer could recall.

The position of the detective was checked so that his position would enable the holes in the back of the overcoat and in the front of the overcoat of the victim to line up with the holes through the upholstering and metal of the car door.

Then the detective took the rifle found in Simmons' possession, held it in a slightly elevated position with the butt of the rifle slightly above the top of the right-hand door, the butt being higher than the muzzle. The muzzle was held in direct contact with the detective's body.

It was evident that Simmons had held the gun in this position, placed the thumb of his right hand on the trigger, and fired the fatal shot, all of the angles and position being maintained with the right-hand door of the car closed. After the shot was fired inflicting the wound which caused death, the gun would be found in the position in which it was found.

"I'm satisfied." Captain Strickland spoke with calm deliberation. "Simmons committed suicide."

Though every factor in this case, with reference to the condition of the body, bore out this verdict, it was the unburned grain of powder found in the lining in the front of the coat that presented the most convincing proof to the layman.

Powder burns often play an important role in determining the condition and cause of violent death. In common parlance, any blackened or dirty area surrounding a bullet hole, caused by the powder burning or the muzzle flash of the gun, is considered as a powder burn. In determining questions relating to powder burns in homicide cases it is necessary to make a differentiation between the types of marks and of what they consist. There are three separate and distinct things which make up what is commonly known as the powder burn.

When the muzzle of the gun is held close to the body, a burn results from the flame or hot gases coming in contact with the skin. This is commonly called a brand.

Then there is a certain amount of smoke, greasy substance, and so on which makes a smudge or blackening around the wound. This is separate and distinct from the brand and is called blackening.

The third element, consisting of fine particles of metal, unburned powder, rust, and dirt, embeds itself in the skin, forming a design not unlike the pattern made by a shotgun. This is called tattooing.

It is, of course, necessary in all cases involving powder burns to take into consideration type and size of gun, as well as the condition of the barrel at the time the gun was fired, whether clean or not.

A recent case of powder burns involved a Colt's .25 automatic pistol. In order to determine the distinctive characteristics of this particular gun, I made a series of experiments using a substance simulating skin and tissue. With the gun held close, a hole with lacerations all around the edge was blown into the object, approximately a half-inch long and the width of the bullet.

The gun held one inch from the object left definite tattooing and powder burns, blackening an area approximately one inch in diameter. Several grains of unburned powder were found inside the simulated wound, the wound being the size of the bullet.

At two and one-half inches there were definite tattooing of powder grains around the wound and definite blackening around the orifice of the wound. Several unburned grains of powder were found as far as three-quarters of an inch from the outside of the wound, the wound being the diameter of the bullet in this instance.

It is by such laboratory experiments that the criminologist determines what may have taken place in a homicide case. Sometimes they tell him from what range a gun was fired; other times, from what angle; what type of ammunition was used, what type of powder. Usually the story is told by the body wound, and this is verified by laboratory experiments arranged under conditions closely resembling those of the crime.

8

MURDER BY THE HEAVENS
BODY WOUNDS — WHAT THEY TELL (CONTINUED)

They who in evil would the gods employ, these the gods destroy!

This proved strikingly true in the case of Arthur Covell. He tried to woo the gods to protect him in a career of crime, but he didn't realize that the gods are never on the side of destructive, antisocial elements. Conversely, they seem to weave a net with which to trap the criminal—a net spun of such flimsy, insignificant things as to catch the malefactor entirely unawares. It is the little thing, seeming almost an act of Providence, that the criminal usually overlooks.

Arthur Covell was familiar with the configurations of the planets; horoscopes told him the secrets of the stars; he sought the aid of the heavens in his diabolical program of murder. But he didn't know that ammonia eventually leaves a burn on dead flesh.

This trifling oversight proved his undoing and was the key that opened the doors on one of the weirdest murder mysteries in my long experience with crime. The murder of Mrs. Ebba Covell involved the strangest man I have ever met—a fiend who resorted to astrology, hypnotism, and some might say sorcery, in planning a series of crimes that would have been the death of many prominent men in Coos County, Oregon, had he not been stopped.

Neither were the local doctors, who conducted the autopsy, familiar with ammonia burns, and this fact almost brought the hangman's noose about the neck of an innocent man—the dead woman's husband.

One morning Dr. Fred Covell, chiropractor of Bandon, Oregon, received a telephone call at his office.

"Come home right away! Something terrible has happened to Ebba!"

Dr. Covell thought it odd that his brother Arthur, who lived with the family, should telephone him, for Arthur Covell was a bedridden invalid who could not walk a step unassisted. However, in his frantic concern for his wife Ebba, he gave the matter little thought.

Then began a wild race through the serene stillness of the Douglas fir forests of Oregon. Nature seems unperturbed by the human tragedies that sear the souls of the few and stir a community and state into flames of passion. When the husband reached his home he found his wife dead, though he tried to revive her. His crippled brother lay upstairs and could give little information, other than that the children had found Mrs. Covell on the floor and he had told them to put her on the bed.

During the inquest a member of the coroner's jury noted that the woman's neck was remarkably loose and free while the rest of the body was stiff (rigor mortis). "It seems to me, her neck is broken," he vouchsafed.

The suggestion was the father of the conviction. The slight incision the doctors made in the back of the neck down the median line was a mere gesture. Everybody was convinced that the neck was broken. Both doctors testified at the inquest she had died from a broken neck. Again we note: "The eyes see in things only what they look for, and they look only for what is already in the mind."

Who could break a neck more easily than the chiropractor with his powerful hands? Dr. Covell was arrested as a suspect.

It was at this stage of developments that Ben Fisher, district attorney of Coos County, called my Seattle office by long-distance telephone and asked me to assist in unraveling the mystery.

I found that the notes taken at the coroner's inquest were very meager, and so I conferred with the physicians who had performed the autopsy. A few pointed questions revealed that, though they were good practicing physicians, they were not familiar with medicolegal autopsies and post-mortems. They had merely made a six-inch incision along the median tine and exposed one or two of the cervical vertebrae. Noting that a finger could be inserted in the spinous process when the head was bent forward, they concluded the neck was broken. This conference made the physicians rather doubtful of their previous conclusions, and, Ben Fisher having given me carte blanche, I ordered the body exhumed for further examination. To assist me, District Attorney Fisher secured the services of Dr. Mingus of Marshfield, Oregon, a man with a wealth of experience gained in coroner's office in Pennsylvania.

This second examination revealed that the neck had not even been dislocated, let alone broken. However, we did find a dark, livid discoloration on the deceased woman's face, to which little importance had been attached at the first autopsy because it did not fit in with the broken neck. Dr. Mingus and I agreed to make separate tests to determine the cause of this discoloration. By the process of elimination, we both determined that the dark red mark on the murdered woman's face had been caused by strong ammonia. This information was kept secret by the doctor, the district attorney, the sheriff's office, and myself.

However, this did not tell us anything about who had applied the ammonia. The previous theory that the neck had been broken by the husband was dissipated. New clues must be found. I had three long conferences with Dr. Covell in his cell and satisfied myself that he was innocent.

We turned to the Covell home. It was obvious that the crippled brother-in-law of the deceased had not committed the crime himself, though he was known to have been at home at the time it occurred. Then there were four children—stepchildren of the deceased. Alton Covell, aged sixteen, had been committed to a school for feeble-minded by a Portland court of domestic relations; but because of crowded quarters at this institution, he had not yet been admitted. The girl, Lucille, fourteen years, seemed not overbright.

Deputy Sheriff Sam Malehorn, who later became assistant fire marshal for the State of Oregon, and made a name for himself as an investigator of arson cases, was assigned to work with me on this case. In the meantime, Alton, the oldest boy, had been arrested as a material witness. In our search of the premises for possible clues we found a diary kept by Arthur Covell, the cripple. It was a peculiar record, for it was written with the aid of astrological signs. Particularly, we became interested in an entry concerning the day of the murder, though it had been entered five days later.

It read: "Made a mistake. Con. wrong—should have subtracted 14 minutes for this latitude and longitude."

The absence of any direct reference in the diary to the death of the sister-in-law seemed significant. He would bear watching. Arthur Covell, we found, was an astrologer of note despite his crippled body. Lying on his bed, he had made an exhaustive study of the pseudo-science of the necromancer. His horoscopes were famous from New York to Hollywood, for we found the horoscopes of many prominent people, including movie stars, in his records.

We also learned his horoscopes had been used by a national syndicate of swindlers to dupe innocent victims. His part was to send the victim a glowing horoscope showing that the stars would be favorable to a very successful investment at a certain time. Another member of the gang would call on the victim at that particular time with an allegedly attractive investment opportunity. It will never be known how many were cheated out of their savings by this device.

While the murder investigation was in progress Arthur Covell had been moved to the County Home, for no one remained at the Covell home to care for him. In the meantime Deputy Sheriff Malehorn learned that the astrologer had placed a box containing some of his horoscopes in the safe-keeping of a neighbor the day he was moved to the County Farm. We had previously searched all through the papers of Dr. Covell for some notation which might be enlightening, but nothing could be found either in the effects of Dr. Covell or among the astrologer's papers.

Taking possession of this box of what appeared to be horoscopes, we found in an envelope a number of slips of paper on which were written what at first seemed to be disconnected plots for stories, and the names of a number of local people appeared thereon. Attached to these slips were other slips bearing astrological characters evenly spaced as though forming words. We decided that this was a cipher code. Together we worked for several days, going over each bit of paper and comparing notes with other bits of paper we found.

Finally we developed a key with which we were able to decipher an intricate code which then enabled us to read the astrological signs which had been used to set down complete instructions to Alton and another nephew to commit a series of crimes.

What we learned astounded us. In it was a list of men and women marked for death. A total of twenty-nine murders had been carefully planned by this cripple, setting out in detail the method and movements to be followed by the boys and what they should do in case the plans should miscarry in any way.

Constellations that governed stellar destinies of these victims showed this fiend the most favorable time at which to strike. And by a man that could hardly lift an arm!

Among the horoscopes was that of Ebba Covell. Apparently she also had been marked as a death victim! But Arthur Covell must have had a confederate—some one who was physically able to carry out his fiendish plans.

In questioning the two oldest children—Alton and Lucille—the district attorney, the deputy sheriff, and I reached the conclusion that these children knew more about the crime than they would admit. A striking feature was the intense, almost passionate love the youngsters had for the uncle— "Uncle Artie," they called him. On the other hand they seemed indifferent to the father's fate. In fact, Lucille said she thought her father had murdered her stepmother.

Mr. Malehorn and I confronted the astrologer at the County Home and told him about our discoveries in his diary and horoscopes.

"Covell," I said, "I have deciphered your code."

For a long minute he did not answer. He looked at me with piercing coal-black eyes—eyes that gleamed with more instinctive animal cunning than any pair of eyes I have ever seen. Later in the interview his eyes kept staring at me with sinister penetration, as though he were trying to hypnotize me. The more I saw of him, the more I realized the weird and uncanny influence he had over the Covell children.

Finally he spoke. "What of it?"

"Just this—you murdered Ebba Covell through the help of your nephew. Your coded notes and horoscopes have told me about your fiendish plans of slaughter. Your plot to kidnap a young Bandon woman, your plan to kill B. J. Pressy, his wife, and three children, are known to us. The will that you so carefully wrote will never be planted on the person of J. Ira Sidwell, and his body with a broken neck will never be found at the bottom of the stairs in his place of business. Your career of crime is at an end; you might just as well confess everything, Covell."

He admitted the planned crimes as yet uncommitted, stating, however, they were only fantasies, but refused to admit any part in killing his sister-in-law.

Alton's complicity was further suspected when it was learned that he had purchased some ammonia about thirty days before the murder. But the boy refused to talk. For two days before the grand jury was to convene to bring in an indictment on the case, Malehorn and I tried to get a confession from Alton Covell on the part he had played in the crime. Always treating him kindly, we tried to reason with him, tried to convince him that he would feel better if he relieved his conscience by making a complete statement.

It seemed all in vain. Then we conceived an idea. By special arrangement we released a story to the newspapers telling about Arthur Covell's admission of having written the planned murders. One newspaper agreed to run a banner headline across the front page, "Crippled Astrologer Plans Murder—Arthur Covell Confesses to Planning Murders." The newspapers were very glad to work with us, for the case had aroused an enormous amount of interest.

As soon as the paper was off the press, I took a copy to Alton Covell. I let him read the headlines; that was all. I didn't care to let him know just what his uncle had confessed.

Yet, despite the fact that the boy thought that his uncle had made a complete confession, he still refused to talk for at least thirty minutes. Instead of having a weak mind, as was generally supposed, it proved that he was unusually strong-minded in a peculiar, warped manner. For instance, the boy had shown unusual cunning in sending messages to his uncle confined at the County Home. His favorite device was to send a magazine to the crippled astrologer, but the sharp eyes of Sheriff Ellingson discovered that the leaves were stuck together. Opening these he found a secret message to the uncle, written on the margin. The uncle responded with a secret message concealed in an apple, placed there after the core had been removed. These messages helped build up evidence against the two confederates.

I was now convinced through a logical process of elimination that Alton Covell was the only one who could have killed his stepmother, and it resolved itself into a battle of wits and a psychological analysis of this peculiar-minded sixteen-year-old boy.

Although only sixteen years of age, he was as large and husky as a man.

Within the innermost depths of almost every one, regardless of how brutal, cold, and indifferent he may outwardly seem, there is a desire to do what looks right to him. I decided to appeal to Alton Covell's better side; and after much entreating and persuasion for him to clear his conscience of this awful deed, carefully following out what I considered his own line of reasoning processes, on the afternoon of October 9, 1928, young Alton Covell gave me his confession while he and I were alone in the sheriff's private office in the courthouse at Coquille, Oregon.

At first he was unable to tell me the gruesome story. I, therefore, asked him to go back to his cell and write it. Malehorn returned him to his cell for the period of an hour. At the expiration of this time he had written nothing except to state on that morning he had found his mother in the kitchen lying on the floor but that he did not know what was the matter with her.

I then told him that he had allowed the bad influences to work against his desire to do what was right and they had overcome his good intentions, and that he should now go back to his cell and write down the truth, in order that he might start life anew with a clean slate even though he had to go to the penitentiary or suffer the extreme penalty.

That I was successful in adopting the line of reasoning which he could understand was borne out by the following confession which he handed me when, at his request, Malehorn brought him back some thirty minutes later:

> I want to start and lead a clean life and I want to be able to look back on everything I do and not be ashamed of anything I will do in the future. I don't know what made me do it. I can't understand why I done such a thing. I will see that it never happens again. I want to look back on a clear trail.
>
> I put the ammonia on the rag and Ebba was standing by the stove. I walked up to her from behind and on the right hand side. I put the rag over her nose with my right hand and held her arms with my left. I held it on her nose for about three minutes after I let her down on the floor. There was a little ammonia left in the bottle and I threw it down into the gulch.
>
> Then I went out and told my uncle that I had done it. Lucille [his sister] and my uncle [the astrologer] knew about the plan first. My uncle was the first to tell me. He told me to get the ammonia and how to use it.

As soon as I had secured the confession from Alton and his signature had been witnessed by Malehorn and Sheriff Ellingson, I went before the grand jury and told them the details. It was agreed that I should now talk to Arthur Covell to see if he would not make a confession either to me or to the grand jury.

Malehorn, Ellingson, Fisher and I drove to the County Farm. On the way out it was decided that I should use the same tactics with Arthur that I used with Alton. Instead of asking Arthur Covell to confess, however, I told him all of the details which I had learned from Alton and showed him the boy's confession in his own handwriting.

I talked with him for some thirty minutes. I did not ask him any questions, merely suggesting what he should do, following the example set by the boy. I told him that the grand jury would see him on the following day and that he should be prepared to tell them the full and complete story.

On the afternoon of October 10, Foreman Matt May of the grand jury closed the door to the little room occupied by Arthur Covell at the County Poor Farm with the bailiff stationed outside to keep away eavesdroppers.

Without waiting for any questions Arthur Covell handed the foreman the following statement which he had already prepared for them:

> I make this as a voluntary statement. I alone was the one to plan the details and select the day. Lucille had nothing to do with the plan or its execution.
>
> Both Alton and Lucille were at all times under control of my mind and will. My will was their will. They never resisted my influence, but done without question as I wished it done. They never argued, or thought if the action was right or wrong, but my influence over both was so complete they seemed incapable to resist or think independently beyond my wish.
>
> In regard to Ebba, soon after moving upstairs, I told Alton I wanted her out of the way. I told him how to do it without violence or bloodshed and with ammonia. I told him I would choose the day, that I would not force him to do it and that if he wanted to refuse it was all right with me; but as I said this, I knew in my own heart he couldn't help doing as I wanted.
>
> My brother Fred is entirely innocent. Lucille is innocent of any participation in the crime. Alton as an individual is innocent. I forced my will on him and made him act for me; in other words I used his body and his strength as

though it were my own, he had not the power of will to resist me. I alone am guilty of the whole thing. I have kept
Alton under my control for a great many years and it is this
which makes him seem not bright, sometimes deficient. My
last instructions to him before we separated was: "If you
get in a tight pinch with this and there is no other way out,
it will be all right with me if you tell how I made you do it.
I do not want you to suffer for my sake." Hence his and my
statement.

Alton has a very mild nature, with nothing vicious in
his makeup and if left to his own devices would be inca-
pable of ever taking a human life.

Arthur Covell.

At the trial Arthur Covell decided to plead "Not guilty." He con-
tended that his confession was made merely to save his nephew.
When that failed of its purpose, he decided to put up a bitter fight
for his life.

Carried into court in the arms of two jail trustees, the defendant seemed cooler and more complacent than anyone else. One
of the ghastliest touches of the trial was supplied by the fourteen-
year-old Lucile. Before going to the witness stand she kissed the
wasted face of her uncle. When the girl had to make answers which
might incriminate Arthur Covell, she would look at him. The uncle
would keep his inscrutable eyes fastened on the child, and she
would be helpless to speak. Not until District Attorney Fisher
stepped between the two, so as to break the spell by which the defendant held the girl mute and helpless, could Lucille answer the
questions asked her.

Defense counsel made the most of the man's physical condition. The story of the accident that had broken Arthur Covell's back,
leaving only a tiny cord of his spinal column to keep life intact and
the brain functioning, was told with appropriate pathos.

But the jury would not be moved. It brought in a verdict of
murder in the first degree.

Alton Covell, the nephew, had been indicted on the same charge and was to be tried separately.

Despite the adverse verdict against him, the astrologer was confident the stars were with him, he declared in his cell. "I will not die for the murder of Ebba Covell. Jupiter, my patron, was in the ascendency, and the sun averse to Venus, Mrs. Covell's patron planet." On this futile hope he appealed the case.

His appeal was denied. The date of his execution was set just eighteen months after his conviction.

Five days earlier Alton Covell went on trial. After forty-five minutes of deliberation the jury agreed that the boy was responsible at the time the crime was committed. He was sentenced to life imprisonment.

But Arthur Covell, whose eyes brightened with mystic zeal as he continued to cast his own horoscope and to study the configurations of the planets in his lonely cell, remained calm and indifferent as he had been at his conviction. At the time he had turned to me, as I stood near his cot, extended his hand, and said: "I carry no ill-will against you; you merely did your duty." When I asked him about the motive for his proposed career of murder, he had said simply: "I am a cripple and didn't want to be dependent on anyone else." The murder of his sister-in-law was prompted by a desire to get rid of her and thus give him the unhampered control of the Covell children.

The execution of this cripple was as gruesome as his own diabolical intrigues. Seated in a wheel chair before the gallows, he was strapped to a board to keep him upright. On this board he went to his doom.

At last the heavens had turned against this man. Truly, they who in evil would the gods employ, them the gods destroy.

One can only guess as to the outcome of the case had I accepted the testimony of the doctors as to the broken neck. The scientific criminologist takes nothing for granted until it can be proved.

9

A Voice from the Grave

In recent reports of a coroner in one of the larger cities of the United States we find a number of statements relevant to suspicious deaths. These statements are almost ludicrous in their significance, and certainly not calculated to inspire much respect for the guardians of public safety. We quote a few of them[1] without comment:

No. 22942: "Could be suicide or murder." [This was the first entry for the year.]
No. 22957: "Auto accident or assault."
No. 23178: "Aunt said she complained of pneumonia; looked like narcotism."
No. 23203: "Believe strychnia used—viewed as suicide."
No. 22964: "Found dead."
No. 22987: "Found dead in shanty."
No. 22990: "Head severed from body."
No. 23035: "Could be assault or diabetes."
No. 23187: "Diabetes, tuberculosis, or nervous indigestion."
No. 23300: "Found dead."
No. 23484: "Found crushed."
No. 23512: "Could be diabetes or poison."

[1] Quoted in "The Coroner and the Medical Examiner," by Oscar T. Schultz and E. M. Morgan, *Bulletin of the National Research Council*, No. 64.

No. 23551: "Died suddenly after taking medicine."
No. 23606: "Died suddenly."

In none of these cases was an autopsy performed to secure more precise information about a specific death to exclude foul play definitely. Apparently it was more convenient to play the old guessing game: "One I love, two I love, three I love the same," et cetera. After all, the daisy's last petal might come as near the truth as necessary in most cases. At least this would not be any more ridiculous than the casual post-mortem examination that is often made.

And this coroner expended $10,771.56 in that year to conduct his office!

The cases cited above are not exceptional. There was the case of "Big Hat"—as he was known to the principals in this case, because he wore one of those ten-gallon sombrero hats on all and every occasion.

He was a prosperous rancher of Idaho and varied the tedium of shearing and tagging sheep by taking flyers in the night life of Mackay. At the time of this story, the little picturesque town of Idaho was wide open with wine, women, and song—take your choice. Ranchers, miners, sheepmen, and cowboys gave zest and color to the village. And some of the happenings were decidedly off-color, for the ancient calling was followed with generous abandon.

One morning Big Hat was found dead across the street from the town's most notorious brothel. Witnesses noted that the man's coat was crushed up under his arms as though he had been recently carried.

The coroner made his examination, and a coroner's jury rendered a verdict that the man had died of natural causes. Though the dead man was a wealthy and prominent rancher of the community, the case was closed officially, and no further investigations made.

Big Hat was buried, and his secret, if such there was, was interred with him.

Two years later, Solon B. Clark was elected prosecuting attorney for Custer County, Idaho. Clark, fresh from law school, and naturally an ambitious young man, sought new worlds to conquer. He knew of the Big Hat case and had always been suspicious of the circumstances surrounding the death of the wealthy rancher. He retained me to start a new investigation secretly. We learned that the stomach of the deceased had been retained by the coroner's physician. It rested undisturbed in its bath of alcohol in the doctor's office.

We decided to investigate further that stomach. But obstacles presented themselves. To request openly that the stomach be submitted would arouse suspicion and probably frustrate any results from a secret investigation of the collateral issues in the case.

But Clark was not only ambitious, but tenacious in his purpose. This unexpected obstacle merely whetted his zeal. Being a resourceful young man, he came into possession of the stomach. Perhaps the less said about the manner of accomplishing this the better, except to say that it was obtained from the doctor's office and another placed in its stead.

Almost like a voice from the grave came the report from Dr. Hartman, a noted toxicologist, that Big Hat had been poisoned. Enough morphine sulphate was found in the man's stomach to kill several people. It is possible that the doctor was innocently ignorant of this fact when he made his report to the coroner. And yet, such a gross error on the part of the coroner should not be dismissed as innocent ignorance.

Immediately upon the discovery of the cause of the man's death we began to trace back the man's movements at the time the crime was committed. We found that in the evening he had visited the Big House, a brothel near which his body was discovered the next morning.

Fortunately we located some of the people who had been inmates of the place at the time. What we learned is contained in affidavits now in my possession. I will present these as they were given to us, not only because of the facts they reveal, but because

of the life they depict—a life that is unknown to most of the readers of this volume. They reveal sordid intrigue in a sordid life, but
are not without human pathos.

We first found a couple of girls who knew of the affair through
a third parry. Their deposition follows, though all names used are
fictitious:

> Ray Moore was running Dot Allen's house at Hailey some
> time last summer, 1914. She called from Hailey for Joe
> Walker by phone at Mackay, and Fred Wells answered the
> 'phone. She thought she was talking to Joe Walker and said,
> "George and May have split up, and May hollered white sla-
> very on George and George says that he is going over, but is
> not going alone, but would spit up his guts about that man,"
> and told him, "For God's sake, come over at once, get an
> automobile and I will pay for it," and Fred said, "This is not
> Joe, it's Fred," and Ray hung up the 'phone receiver with-
> out saying another word.
>
> The George she meant is George Lander. May went by the
> name of May Johnson, and both had been in Mackay when
> the man was found dead near Lyon's office some time ago.
>
> Fred Wells told us about this. That is the way we know.

This disconnected statement told us many things.

Most interesting to us was the fact that a woman by the name
of Ray Moore became wildly disturbed when she learned that a
lovers' quarrel might reveal a hidden secret about a man. We knew
that this Ray Moore had been the landlady in the Big House at the
time of the murder.

Joe Walker apparently was the confidant of this woman and
perhaps a confederate in the vicious murder.

Another signed statement brought us closer to the truth. It was
given by another girl. It follows:

> Georgie Smith told me that she was in a room in Ray
> Moore's house at Mackay, and Ray and a girl named Mamie

Regan were in an adjoining room talking, and she, Georgie, overheard the conversation. Georgie heard Ray say to Mamie, "Don't you think that May is a dirty s— b—; after I doped that guy and killed him she only gave me $50.00. I didn't mean to kill him, but I was drunk and I gave him too much." Mamie answered, "I'd have knocked her on the head and took it." And Ray said: "What could I do, she had me." Ray also said that Joe Walker and George Lander carried the doped man out. This was about a week after the man was found dead near Lyon's office in Mackay about two years ago.

We found Georgie Smith, and this girl verified the above statement. However, all this was hearsay and we had to find some of the principals directly involved. The girl Mamie Regan was located in Ketchum, and after seeing the evidence we had obtained she reluctantly gave a complete story of the vicious killing at the brothel:

On the night of September 22nd, 1913, about 7 o'clock in the evening, a little sheep herder came into the Big House where I was working, and sat around there for a while, and had a few drinks and danced around with me a while in the dance hall. The drinks were served by Ray Moore, the landlady of the house. Then I took the gentleman up to my room, and he offered me two dollars to stay with me. I refused it and said that I was not in the habit of taking two dollars, instead of three dollars. Then he said he was a tough guy and that he would kill me; said that he had a gun in his pocket. I told him I didn't want any trouble. Then he wanted me to understand that he had more money than I thought he had, and he pulled a blue piece of paper out of his pocket and put it on the dresser. I told him to put it back in his pocket and to come downstairs and have a drink. We went downstairs and had another dance, and more drinks. Ray Moore said that she was going to "dope" him and get his money. May and I were together when she said this. She served drinks to us and she handed him one, and although I did not see her put the "dope" in it, it is my understanding that the drink he got had the dope in it.

A short time after this drink I went to the parlor, known as the Red Room, and he was lying down on the couch, and he looked like he was all in and down and out. He looked green and yellow in the face; his eyes were closed, and he was breathing heavily, kind of a choking sound like he was choking to death. Then Ray called George Lander and Joe Walker, "For God's sake, I have given him too much dope; take him out and don't let him die in the house."

As they started to take him out, I was standing in the Red Room door, and I took one look at him and ran into the side parlor and then turned out the front light while the men took him out.

The next morning May and I were in bed together when Ray came to the door and said, "My God, girls, that fellow is dead." She told us not to be scared, that she had destroyed the dope in the toilet. She urged us to stay by her, and that if we didn't she would kill us, and it was because of this that I testified at the inquest that the man had gone out of the front door and never come back.

When I was arrested on the 27th day of March, 1915, she told me to tell that Joe Walker had sit on the couch in the parlor and say that if she didn't give him money that he would tell on her. While in the custody of the Sheriff at the Terrell Hotel I was talking to Ray and she said not to tell only what I had to and that Joe Walker was doing this for money (squealing) and she said for God's sake to stick by her. I asked if she thought that May and George Lander would stay by her, and she said, "yes." She said that she never would give in and that she would fight it out.

We have talked this matter over several times, that is, Ray Moore and myself, wherein she stated that she had killed him by an over-dose of dope which she put in his drink. She often asked me if I ever had told anyone, and she said if I ever did that she would kill me. I have known her to previously dope people, and she told me that she had to be awful careful and not give them too much, because it might kill them. After she had killed this man, he was known around the house as "Big Hat." Once, when she was in Hailey she got a telephone call from Joe Walker at Mackay, saying over the telephone something about "The Big Hat," and she told central that if he should call up again not to call her for he was crazy. Later she called me at Johnny Anderson's saloon in Ketchum, saying that Joe Walker and she thought May and George too were going to squeal on her.

A gnawing conscience, a morbid fear of detection, threatened blackmail, all played a part in making the life of Ray Moore a hell on earth.

The statement by Joe Walker is not without its humorous aspects. It mentions casually a "business transaction" where principals haggled over the price of love! And where bartering frugality brought death. Walker's role of "Cook for one Nettie Schofield" may bring a smile, but withal it is humor amid grim tragedy!

Joe Walker, by the way, designated himself as pianist for Ray Moore's brothel. His statement, secured from him in Salmon, Idaho, after much questioning, follows:

One night of September, 1913, I was working as usual at The Big House in Mackay and was at the piano when I was called into the Red Parlor about nine thirty. There I found, upon entering the parlor, a man lying in a semi-conscious condition, apparently intoxicated. He was lying upon a couch. I found him lying there to my knowledge dead to the world, seemingly intoxicated. I was requested to pick him up and carry him out which I did with the assistance of one George Lander, and this all happened between nine thirty and ten o'clock.

I was requested by Ray Moore, landlady, and one May Johnson, inmate of the house so to do. We picked him up and carried him over across the street and set him down by a fence post at the corner, in the north corner of the lumber yard. I went back into the house and left again at twelve o'clock, going to my room. The first I heard anything was wrong was about ten o'clock the next morning. The only thing I remember was that he wore a big hat. He was short, and weighed, I should judge, about one hundred eighty-five or ninety pounds. This was the first and only time I ever saw him.

When we laid the man down, I tried his pulse and I also listened to his heart and from my judgment he was in perfect health. He came into the house somewhere between eight and nine-thirty. He had some words with one Mamie Regan, another inmate of the house over a business transaction and when he came down was the time I was called. When I was paid off that night, I understood from the talk, indirectly, that Ray Moore had given him a shot of dope, and rolled him for $250, though May Johnson got the bulk of the money. I had heard prior to my employment in this house that it was the custom of this mistress, Ray Moore, to dope men for their money. I know personally that a miner from the hills came to that house and was robbed of somewhere between two-hundred and three-hundred dollars, he also being under the influence of dope at the time.

During this business proposition with Mamie Regan the stipulated price was three dollars and my understanding was that he only had two dollars to pay. However, I learned he had displayed his roll to one of the inmates.

I was out camping in July, cooking for one Nettie Schofield and I heard it rumored that there would be an attempt to make trouble for Ray Moore, by accusing her of the murder of this man, and upon my return I called up Ray Moore but I couldn't get any satisfaction over the telephone, so I wrote her a letter and I stated that cause just as I had heard it, that they were trying to make trouble for her. She wrote back to me and told me for God's sake to end this suspense and come and see her immediately. I did not go and wrote another letter.

Ray Moore was arrested in Hailey, where she was operating a house of ill fame. Her real name proved to be Margaret Conway, and it was easy to see that once she had been a beautiful woman. It was said that she had once been an artist's model in Chicago. She was still a young woman at the time of her arrest—about twenty-eight years old, but years of dissipation had taken their toll.

A rather pathetic development of the case was the finding of George Lander and May Johnson. They were finally located on a small farm near Ogden, Utah. There they had bought a small piece of ground and were making a valiant effort to live down the past. They had forsaken the life of the brothel and were now tilling the soil for a livelihood, apparently happy and contented. For all I know they may have returned there and may now be respected members of the community.

The principal never came to trial on this earth, for the day prior to her trial Margaret Conway, alias Ray Moore, committed suicide in the cell she occupied in the Custer County jail.

And thus ended a case that might have been less of a murder mystery if a country coroner had not failed in his duty.

10
The Eternal Triangle

In the preceding three chapters it is obvious that the body of a victim of violent death plays a major role. That is true in every homicide case and this is never more evident than when the body of a person presumably murdered cannot be found.

Without the physical evidence of the *corpus delicti* it is impossible to convict an individual for murder in most states. Regardless of how impressive the circumstantial evidence in the case may be, the missing body of the victim thwarts every effort to build up a case for conviction. The only way to prove that murder has been committed is to produce the dead body. The shrewd criminal knows this and often he uses diabolical cleverness to conceal the body, defying the most exhaustive efforts of the authorities.

There is the historic case of Decasto Mayer, who, everybody familiar with the case is convinced, murdered Eugene Bassett, a naval officer of the Bremerton Navy Yard. Yet, his body was never found despite region-wide search by several posses over a period of several months. Clairvoyants and spiritualistic mediums gave the authorities the usual run of false leads. "Truth serum" was administered without success in this particular case. The Lie Detector was employed, but Mayer refused to go on with the tests when it started to reveal his inner emotions, and he smashed the instrument before the location of the body was determined. No murder charge was made, but the man was convicted of stealing the missing man's automobile and sentenced to life imprisonment as an habitual criminal.

The Richard Connor murder case threatened to be a similar mystery. It involved the eternal triangle wherein the passions of illicit love stirred the murderer to a singularly cold-blooded killing of his wife. It has been said that the primitive emotion of sex in some form or manifestation—either thwarted love or jealousy—holds a leading rank as a motivating influence to murder. Avarice, or the acquisitive instinct of man, is perhaps entitled to first place in furnishing the motives for all manner of crimes, including murder. The Connor case involved both these primal instincts, which, in this case, produced a fiendish brutality and cunning rarely encountered.

It was in May during the first burst of spring that Richard Connor took his wife for her last drive through the beautifully wooded country that she had known since girlhood. Mrs. Pearl R. Connor had often taken these rides in the country with her husband. This occasion, however, was more auspicious, for Pearl Connor was to learn to drive the family automobile.

They left their home near Spanaway, Washington, at dusk. Mrs. Connor never returned. To her it was a ride of death.

It was several days before her absence was known to relatives and friends. Richard Connor first reported his wife's absence to her parents who lived less than a dozen miles away. Though he told what to him seemed a plausible story, the parents became frantic with anxiety and reported the case to authorities.

Connor related how he and his wife had made an extended drive by automobile through the region, and finally he had turned the motor car toward the home of Mrs. Connor's parents. When within half a mile of this place, the wife had asked him to stop the car, saying that she wanted to visit her parents' home, and that she would walk the rest of the distance. He told how she had kissed him and had started walking up the road. Turning his car around, the husband had started for home.

By careful insinuations the man tried to convince authorities that his wife had run away with another man. He casually told officials that a Chevrolet sedan had been parked a short distance from the place where he had left his wife.

But these implications did not stop the hue and cry for the missing woman. In all her thirteen years of married life Pearl Connor had never had an extramarital affair with any man, friends testified. She was not the kind of woman whom one would expect to make a spectacular elopement with a lover. Connor's story didn't ring true.

Then it was known that Mrs. Connor had filed suit for divorce about three weeks earlier, charging her husband with cruelty and keeping company with other women. Just a week before the woman disappeared, this suit was dismissed by stipulation, and Connor declared that all marital differences had been ironed out, and that they had been happy since the reconciliation.

The charge in the divorce suit prompted officials to look for the "woman in the case." One of my assistants found her in the person of—let us call her Mrs. Knight. Continued investigation disclosed that Connor had had a rendezvous with this woman at an Olympia resort the day after his wife disappeared. Instead of searching frantically for the missing wife, he had callously gone off on a party with his mistress! Selden and I arranged to confront her with our findings; she readily admitted her liaison with Connor, but protested that she knew nothing about his wife's disappearance. We were, however, able to convince her that Connor must have been instrumental in his wife's disappearance, whereupon she furnished us with the information that Connor had met her the same night his wife disappeared.

However, the strongest suspicion of foul play was aroused at the time Prosecuting Attorney J. W. Selden and I searched the Connor home. There we found the missing woman's wardrobe, and it was complete in every particular. All the intimate items of apparel that a woman loves, her toilet articles and fineries that she would certainly have taken with her on any trip, were still in her boudoir. This convinced us that Mrs. Connor had not run away with another man as the husband intimated.

Then another woman came into the case—whom we will call Ethel Bernhardt, a lifelong friend of Mrs. Connor, and also a friend of Prosecuting Attorney Selden. At the latter's suggestion, Mrs.

Bernhardt agreed to help the authorities solve the baffling disappearance of her friend.

Mrs. Bernhardt proved herself an astute amateur detective. In order to win Connor's confidence she told him that she would inform the authorities that she had seen Mrs. Connor and another man in a Chevrolet sedan in Oregon going south on a highway leading toward California.

At this point Connor made a serious mistake. He agreed to this deception—in fact, welcomed it.

"But why don't we do a good job of this?" he asked Mrs. Bernhardt. "Why don't you write a letter to me, supposedly coming from my wife, telling me that she has run away with a man, and is now in California?"

Mrs. Bernhardt agreed. She secured a specimen of Mrs. Connor's handwriting from a recipe book, and forged a letter presumably from the missing wife.

Connor triumphantly showed it to Mr. Selden, hoping thereby to call off the search for his missing wife. However, this overt act of deception resulted in Connor's arrest. So strong was the public feeling against him that Sheriff Desmond of Pierce County took the precaution of transferring the prisoner to Vancouver, Washington, in an adjacent county.

The search for the body continued with increased vigor; several posses practically covered every foot of ground for miles around.

In the meantime a second episode in this drama was taking place in the Clarke County jail. In an effort to make Connor reveal where he had hidden the body of his wife, Sheriff Desmond took Mrs. Bernhardt to Vancouver to interview the prisoner.

The stage was carefully set. Prosecuting Attorney Hall of Clarke County and the sheriff, Mr. Thompson, played initial roles. In the presence of the prisoner they argued about the right of the visiting woman to see Connor.

"I'm satisfied this woman is a sister of Connor," Hall said to the sheriff. "She has come all the way from California, and we ought to let her see him."

"Well, I can't let anyone see him without an order," the sheriff countered.

"You don't need an order in the case of relatives," Hall assured the sheriff.

With seeming reluctance the sheriff agreed to let Mrs. Bernhardt visit Connor in his cell. There she remained forty minutes. In view of the fact that Connor's whereabouts was not known to the general public, Mrs. Bernhardt had to give an explanation of how she learned of his presence in Vancouver. This she did by telling Connor that a prominent business man of Tacoma had used his influence with the superior court judge to learn where the prisoner was hidden.

Connor swallowed this story hook, line, and sinker. He appeared very happy to see Mrs. Bernhardt, so happy in fact that even in the dismal confines of his cell, with his life threatened by the hangman's noose, he tried to make love to his feminine visitor! Human callousness sometimes passes understanding!

"Now, Dick," Mrs. Bernhardt declared, "they've organized a big searching party and will cover the entire county. I'm sure they'll find the body soon. If you want me to help you further, you'll have to tell me where the body is so I can go there and plant evidence. I'll tell them that the man I saw with Mrs. Connor in the Chevrolet wore goggles. I'll leave some goggles there and also a Chevrolet hub cap. They'll think this man killed her."

"That's the finest thing I've heard," Connor replied enthusiastically. "Also get a Luger pistol—a rusty one. Fire one shot and then throw it down.

"You know, Ethel, I didn't kill Pearl. She got out of the car and drew a gun. She fired one shot at me but missed and then killed herself."

"For goodness' sake, Dick, why didn't you take the body home and explain that to the authorities?"

"Nobody would believe me: I'd be the goat and get arrested for murder. So I took her body to an old well near the Mount Rainier road and threw it in."

Connor then detailed how Mrs. Bernhardt could find the abandoned well.

Officers soon located this well on the Camp Lewis Military reservation. It had been filled in with old logs and the sides caved in, and that accounted for the fact that three weeks earlier this identical well had been examined by Mrs. Connor's father and two brothers without result.

Men worked all night to clear away the debris, and curb the sides of the well before the body was recovered. Near the well a shell was found for a 7.65 Luger Automatic pistol—the type of gun found in the Connor home at the time the place was searched. A number of full metal patch cartridges had been found with Connor's gun at the time I searched the house.

Laboratory tests revealed that the shell found at the scene of the crime had been fired by Connor's pistol.

The body wound also verified this contention and also exploded Connor's contention that his wife had shot herself. An examination of the skull showed two bullet wounds, one at the base of the skull and the other at the hair line on the forehead.

The wound at the base of the skull was definitely determined to have been the wound of entrance. It measured 0.31 of an inch in diameter, which is the nominal calibre and would be the size of a wound made by a 7.65 Luger pistol. Furthermore, the interior of this wound showed a conical opening, gradually expanding and becoming larger on the inside.

The wound of exit also bore evidence of being inflicted by a full metal patched bullet, for in no place was the wound wider than the diameter of a 7.65 calibre Luger pistol. It was further proved in the laboratory that only a full metal patched bullet with a velocity similar to that of the Luger could have penetrated through the skull at that particular point. A lead bullet would have torn a much larger hole at the point of exit, as would a soft-nosed bullet.

Obviously the woman could not have shot herself at the base of the skull.

All this evidence was presented to the jury by United States District Attorney Thomas P. Revelle and Wallace Mount, the case going to a federal court because the body had been found on government ground.

It was a hard-fought case, but the jury was convinced that Connor had killed his wife rather than divide their property in divorce proceedings. His affair with Mrs. Knight was admitted.

But the pertinent fact is that the body of the murdered woman was the major thing that brought conviction. It revealed that she had not eloped with another man; that she had not committed suicide; but that she had been shot with a Luger pistol, and that pistol belonged to Richard Connor, her husband.

He paid the penalty with life imprisonment in the United States Penitentiary at Leavenworth, Kansas.

11

HAIRS AND FIBRES IN CRIME DETECTION

A woman was shot by an unknown assailant as she surprised a burglar at work. Seeking the source of a noise which had awakened her, she walked down the hall, and as she passed the door she was shot, the person doing the shooting stumbling over her body as he rushed through the door to make his escape.

As is the case with so many crimes where bits of clothing or wearing apparel are left at the scene of the crime, in this instance the burglar lost his cap on making his egress through a window.

A number of young men in the neighborhood were suspected and arrested. The cap was submitted to my laboratory for examination. It was but a matter of moments to eliminate all of the young men who had been under suspicion, for three hairs were found in the cap, and these hairs were determined to be of negroid origin. This report given to the detectives started a search by them among a group of negroes. A general round-up of this gang was made, and as a result several guns were found, all of which were sent to the laboratory at my request. One of these was established definitely as the gun which had fired the fatal bullet. However, it was the hair that furnished the initial clue that resulted in the subsequent apprehension of the criminal.

Though striking as this celebrated case may be, it does not reveal half of what a criminologist can do in reconstructing a crime from a tiny bit of hair.

The Nemesis of the criminal is often a single hair suspending a Damoclean sword of vengeance.

Hair can tell the criminologist a great many things. Not only can he differentiate between human and animal hair, but he can determine from what part of the human body a particular hair originates. However, exhaustive research must precede any such determinations, for, as in other sciences, a little learning is a dangerous thing.

He can determine the race and approximate age of an individual by examining the hair.

He knows whether a hair has been cut, shaved, or torn out of the body violently.

He can tell whether or not the hair has been subjected to dye.

The recent use of "black light," or ultraviolet rays, now enables him to determine even the brand of dye or pomade used on hair. The use of "black light" in crime detection will be discussed in a subsequent chapter.

The use of invisible rays enables the criminologist in many cases to identify an individual by his hair, as human hair glows in different colors when seen under the penetrating violet ray. It has been discovered that hair from the head of a natural blonde may fluoresce with a dozen different hues, but that from a bleached blonde will always shine with the same bluish glow.

Hair has always been a prolific source of evidence when found on clothing, although often it is overlooked. The hackneyed illustration of the proverbial blond hair found on the husband of a brunette is nevertheless pertinent. But we advise the brunette wife to be circumspect, for the innocent husband may have picked the blond hair from the back of an upholstered chair at the hotel.

Following are thumbnail sketches of a number of my cases wherein hairs and fibres figured in the detection and conviction of the criminal:

The long blond hairs on a shovel were proved to correspond to that of the victim, who had been buried in a barnyard. The shovel was also identified as the weapon used to crush the skull by the hair matted in blood at the point where the shovel joined the wooden handle.

A knife was found, belonging to a suspect, and on it were certain cotton fibres imbedded in blood. In cutting the throat of his victim, the murderer had also cut through the colored collar. The identity in color and structure of the fibres on the knife and those of the collar were conclusively proved.

Near the scene of a crime was found an axe which the suspect stated had been used in killing a calf by striking it on the head. A microscopic examination showed the hair on the axe to be human hair, and it was later proved that the axe had been used in committing a homicide.

A bit of wool imbedded in animal grease and certain vegetable fibres found on the interior of a gun picked up near the scene of murder revealed to authorities that the gun had once belonged to a sheep herder in a certain section of Idaho where this vegetable is native. Through the search in that particular region, the gun was traced to the two men who committed the crime.

Small hairs were found near the handle on the blade of a pocket-knife taken from a suspect. These hairs were identified as coming from the hide of a calf found buried in a field. The calf had been stolen, and the hair of the animal was the evidence that convicted the man.

A woman assaulted in a dark room at night in resisting the intruder pulled several strands of hair from his head. This hair, later found on the carpet by the investigator, enabled him to obtain an approximate description, which brought about the arrest and identification of a suspect.

Woolen fibres found adhering to a splinter on a window sill resulted in a description of the clothing worn by a burglar. He was arrested and convicted on this tiny bit of evidence.

In cases of rape, the examination of the hairs about the female genitals may reveal the existence of spermatozoa, which cling to them with remarkable tenacity, even to resisting ordinary washing, unless performed before the seminal secretion has had time to dry. Moreover, loose hairs corresponding to those of the accused may be found on the victim and hairs corresponding to those of the victim on the accused, thus furnishing material evidence.

It is indeed surprising the number of details the investigator may determine from the examination of hair. The laboratory technique is often involved. In the laboratory, I have hundreds of microscopic slides on which are mounted the better known fibres, animal hair, and hair from various parts of the human body and at various ages. This enables the examiner to come to a conclusion at short notice and also gives him an actual knowledge of the structure and peculiarities of different hairs. He does the same with fibres—cotton, wool, flax, jute, silk, rayon, and many others gathered from all corners of the world. Sometimes it is possible to tell in what particular country the fibre and clothing originated.

Likewise, many determinations and details may be obtained through analysis of certain elements in the structure of human hair which were hitherto believed to be of only secondary and negligible importance. Often of great consequence in the expert's examination is the element called "pigment" which is usually distributed within the compact cells of the cortex and is composed of tiny granules of regular size, shape, and color. The pertinent thing is that this element varies according to the racial origin of the owner of the hair. The hairs of different races have certain special characteristics.

Human hair also has the remarkable faculty of absorbing odors, gases, et cetera, and retaining them for comparatively long periods. This is important when it is desired to determine whether a man, dead or alive, at the moment of examination, had been in a place impregnated with a gas or smell. This may often be the crux of an investigation.

The criminal investigator takes every precaution to preserve hairs found at the scene of a crime. He keeps them sterile by picking them up with tweezers and placing them, if possible, in hermetically sealed test tubes. He notes carefully the conditions under which the hair is found. Later it is inspected and any adherent particles are preserved. Then it is washed, dried, and mounted in suitable media for examination. In some tests, reagents are introduced to determine the identity of different hairs and fibres by color changes and solubility. Biological tests have demonstrated the possibility of developing a technique for identification by this means.

Though the technique is not important to the layman, it is, nevertheless, interesting to know that human hair can usually be distinguished from that of the lower animals by its structure. Microscopical comparison of human hairs with those of lower animals, in nearly all cases shows definite distinguishing characteristic features of cuticle, medulla, and cortex. The cuticle of human hair, which is composed of very fine scales projecting very slightly, can be detected only by careful focusing with a high-powered lens and only after the hair has been thoroughly cleansed.

Animal hairs, on the other hand, yield a very characteristic appearance, especially evident when any excess of pigment is dissolved in strong acid, in that they are composed of much larger scales which project prominently in steplike or wavy succession. The greater breadth of the medulla of animal hairs is another distinguishing characteristic that aids the examiner in determining whether a certain hair is human or animal. The varying cellular structure of hair of different animals enables the expert to determine from what animal a particular hair came.

Likewise the hairs of different races can be distinguished, one from another. Suffice it to say that the cross-section structure of human hair is one of the most helpful factors in this determination. The general principle is, "The rounder the hair (cross-sectionally) the stiffer and straighter." Also, hair generally curls in proportion to its flatness, or ellipticity, the latter being the characteristics of the Papuans, the former of the yellow race. In other words, the races with kinky or curly hair are identified by means of their elliptical or kidney-shaped hair, while the American Indians and the yellow race are distinguished by hair that in cross-section is almost round. The hair of the white race presents an oval cross-section under the microscope. Of course, there are other determining factors with which we need not concern ourselves in this volume.

The experts can, within certain limits, determine the age of the person by examining some of his hair. This is relatively simple if the hair still has its roots intact. The roots of the hair dissolve in a solution of caustic potash, and in making such tests the length of time this process requires determines the approximate age when properly carried out with suitable standards. The younger the individual, the more quickly the roots dissolve. In very young children the roots dissolve almost immediately, while in very old people the process may require several hours, depending upon the technique used. Previous tests with hair from individuals of known age make possible a fairly accurate scale of ages depending on the time element of dissolution. Examination of pigmentary cells also tells a story of age.

Unfortunately science has not reached the stage where an expert can definitely and positively identify a hair as coming from a particular individual, though the fluorescence of hair under "black light" enables him to come very close to this. There are too many qualifying factors involved.

12
A Hair Brings Vengeance
(Hairs and Fibres Continued)

Often the innocence or guilt of a suspect depends upon what the expert finds out about a bit of hair. Sometimes it is necessary to determine not only that the hair in question is human hair, but from what portion of the body it came.

The different variations in length, thickness, and form of human hair will usually indicate the region of the body from which the hair came, provided it appears in sufficient quantities. When only a single hair is found, the conclusion may often be uncertain.

The fine downy hairs that cover the surface of the body can be identified by their fineness, shortness, and absence of medulla and pigment. The hairs of the pubes, axilla, and chest vary in length from one to three inches, while shorter hairs suggest an origin from the regions of the arms and legs. Eyebrows, lashes, and nostrils have hairs from one-fourth to three-fourths of an inch in length.

Hairs from different parts of the body differ in their diametrical measurements; also hair varies with the age and type of the individual. Hairs in the same region vary greatly in different individuals, and even in the same individual, when diametrical measurements are taken.

If the hair of an individual is straight, the cross-section will appear round or circular. This is true of the eyelashes and straight hair found on the scalp, while hair on the pubes, beard, chest, axilla, is twisted and curly, presenting a triangular or irregular cross-section.

Hair roots cleansed in strong alkali appear short and thick in the case of long body hairs; the short body hairs have a long thin root; and the roots of the beard and the head hairs lie between these extremes, being a little longer than broad.

The short hairs from the nares and eyelashes come to a point very rapidly while the larger hairs slowly diminish in diameter toward their tips, being extremely minute for a short distance from the tip. The body hairs have rounded ends, sometimes being split or thickened because of the friction they are subjected to by the clothing and the perspiration of the body.

Hairs of the scrotum, vulva, and axilla are constantly subjected to moisture and rubbing.

The pubic hairs are generally oval and much flattened and often present considerable roughness.

The hairs of the eyebrows are usually firm at the point, smooth, angular, or oval on section, and possess a stout knoblike bulb. The eyelashes have spindle-shaped roots, and hairs from the nose and ears are coarser in structure and have stout roots.

This analysis of the nature of human hair may mean little to the average layman, but to the criminal investigator the success or failure of a case may depend on such knowledge. Many a criminal has met his doom because of a few tiny hairs.

There is the case of James Woodin, whose conviction for first-degree murder depended on the identification of a few hairs found on a piece of stove wood as coming from the eyebrow of the murdered man. These few eyebrow hairs gave the lie to the first statement of the accused that the killing had been accidental.

Allen Presley was an elderly recluse who lived alone near McCue, Washington. A few days before the Christmas of 1927, his body was found in his home by neighbors. Apparently the man had been dead for some time, for the body was frozen as it lay hidden under the cot where the murderer had put it.

Murder it certainly was, local authorities concluded, for the man had a bullet wound in one eye, and no weapon was in evidence to give a suggestion of possible suicide. There was no money on the man's person, which indicated a possible robbery motive.

After careful questioning of all the neighbors it was learned that James Woodin, a youngster in his late teens, had been hunting rabbits in that neighborhood four days earlier. Furthermore, he had been seen going into the yard of the Presley home, carrying his gun with him.

Local authorities followed up this clue, locating young Woodin on a farm near an adjacent town where he was employed. At first he denied all knowledge of the shooting, but later he admitted that it had been an accident.

"I went to old Presley's place early in the afternoon," he declared, "and gave the old man a couple of rabbits I had shot. Then I left but came back in the evening just before train time, for I wanted to leave my gun with Presley. Just as I handed him the gun it went off, the bullet hitting him in the head.

"Then I got scared and pushed his body under the cot, and covered his head with an old coat."

That was as much as the public learned about the case until it came to trial, a little over a month later. In the meantime we had found several very incriminating bits of evidence in the Presley home.

There was a grim tenseness in the court room when young Woodin was brought up for trial. He was well known in the community, and his youth brought the accused many sympathizers who could hardly believe that such an atrocious killing by one so young was possible.

Weather-beaten farmers, stirred from the peaceful routine of a well-ordered life in this uneventful community, crowded the courtroom. The boy whose life was in pawn, and who previously had been so complacent, appeared to sense the tragedy that stalked him, for his cold indifference was gone as he twisted and squirmed in his seat. Endlessly he made nervous scribblings on a sheet of paper.

To most of the onlookers he was "Jim," a small boy hidden between a towering deputy and a bulky attorney. The mere mention of "capital punishment" by defense attorneys in questioning prospective jurors brought gray agony to the young man's face. Too late he realized that his rash act would inexorably drive him to the brink of eternity, and, perhaps, hurl him to the bottomless pit from which there is no return.

When the routine testimony had been heard relevant to Woodin's presence at the Presley home at about the time of his death, physical evidence of the prosecution was presented. It was in the nature of a piece of stove wood found at the scene of the crime.

The shell of a .22 cartridge had also been found in the room where the man was murdered, and this was shown conclusively, by means of large photomicrographs which I had prepared, to have been fired from the gun owned by Woodin. This point was not contested, for the accused had already admitted that this bullet from his gun had killed Presley. The defense claimed it was an accidental killing.

But the piece of stove wood told a different story. On this piece of wood was a small stain of human blood with a few hairs adhering to human tissue. Also there was a grain of unburned powder on the wood near the stain.

Previous laboratory tests had shown this stain to be that of human blood; the hairs proved to be from a human eyebrow, being firm at the point, smooth, and round in cross-section, and possessing stout, knoblike roots. Examination showed that there were three distinct shades of hair on the piece of wood, and similar shades of hair were found on Presley's eyebrows.

The condition of the body indicated that, besides the bullet wound in his eye, the skull was fractured in this region, and the wound gave evidence of having been inflicted by a heavy blow from a blunt instrument. However, the latter assumption was not entirely obvious because the bullet wound and the blow wound were in an identical place.

On the witness stand I was interrogated as to these findings. When I had finished, the defense counsel turned to me and did not even try to conceal the sneer in his voice as he asked, "Now just what do you deduce from all these learned expositions?"

I hesitated a moment before answering, for it is never the prerogative of an expert witness to make any personal deductions. It is his sole duty to present facts as he finds them, and then let the jury make what deductions they may. However, when I was asked for my opinion I was forced to give it, however much it might disconcert the defense. The State would not be allowed to ask such a question.

"I deduce that this particular gun fired the bullet found in Allen Presley's head. This shot was first fired, and then the assailant picked up a stick of stove wood and hit the victim with it on the eyebrow, crushing his skull to make sure of his death."

The presence of the unburned grains of powder on the stick showed conclusively that the bullet wound had been inflicted before the blow was struck.

These findings exploded the accident theory, and the jury brought in a verdict of guilty and recommended life imprisonment. The boy had planned the murder and robbed the victim of $37.50 with which to buy a Christmas present for his girl.

A life sold for a mere pittance!

13
A CAR OF DEATH
(HAIRS AND FIBRES CONTINUED)

Thurlow Hudlow, farmer of Okanogan County, Washington, met a fate that is much too common in these days of fast motor transportation. Reckless automobile driving is a major curse of a motorized civilization.

But this farmer whose life was snuffed out on a busy street of Tacoma, Washington, by a driver in a terrific hurry to get nowhere in particular, was avenged. A few hairs found on the fender of the death car brought its driver a just conviction.

There is nothing glamorous nor mysterious about an automobile tragedy; it is so commonplace as to create little interest. Unlike a baffling murder by an unknown and sinister assailant, the victim of ruthless driving draws a street crowd, perhaps, and then the incident is forgotten.

Yet, this case is noteworthy as an example of the major role that human hair sometimes plays in the detection and conviction of criminals.

It was a rainy night in early fall when Hudlow began to cross Jefferson Street, Tacoma, confused, perhaps, by unfamiliar city noises. At any rate he did not see the speeding, weaving automobile that was rushing toward him.

Smash! And it was all over for Thurlow Hudlow.

The death car continued its furious pace, but fortunately a traffic officer got a fleeting glance at the car and noted its make in the dusk. The number was not visible.

Death came almost instantly to the victim. Examining his body next day at the morgue, I found that the skull had been fractured; and various body bruises gave evidence of the terrible impact he had suffered.

Forty-five minutes after the man had been hit police found a suspected car several blocks away. Obviously there could be little more than suspicion, for a hasty glance at a speeding automobile is subject to error, and hundreds of similar automobiles could be found in Tacoma. However, the officer's identification of the car was supported by indications that it had been in an accident.

Sam Long, owner of the car, was soon found by the capable officer in a restaurant near where it was parked. He was arrested and charged with manslaughter. Later it was learned that the man had been drinking, which is usually the case with reckless drivers.

After examining the body of the deceased and noting the relative position of all body wounds, I investigated the automobile in question. On the right fender of this automobile there appeared a crescent-shaped, jagged, sharp opening in the sheet-metal at the side of a depression. This depression in the fender would conform to an impression such as would be made by the back of a man's head forcibly striking the thin sheet-metal apron.

This mark on the automobile seemed very pertinent, for an examination of Hudlow had disclosed a semi-circular wound corresponding in size and shape with the jagged, sharp opening in the fender. The bumper of the automobile also revealed that it had suffered a hard blow on the right side. This explained bruises found on the legs of the deceased at the same relative distance as the height of the bumper from the ground.

However, the most damning bit of evidence against the automobile and its owner was a number of short strands of hair with a minute particle of flesh adhering to them.

Examination disclosed that this particle of flesh was comparatively fresh, but more pertinent was the fact that the hair proved to be human hair, identical in color and structure to hair taken from the orifice of the wound on the head of the deceased.

Science can rarely, if ever, positively identify a strand of hair as coming from a particular individual by color and structure alone. Theoretically no two things in the world are exactly alike in every particular, including the hair of two individuals. But in the case of human hair the similarity at times is so striking as to preclude a positive generalization.

However, sometimes there is a supplementing factor that makes identification of hair practically positive—as positive as most things can be. This is adherent matter—dirt if you will. After all, dirt is merely misplaced matter.

This additional factor of adhering particles of foreign matter made identification of the hair found on the fender as coming from the head of the deceased virtually positive. Both specimens of hair, that found on the gash in the fender and that taken from the head of the deceased, revealed identical foreign matter—dust particles of a similar nature.

Though no one could identify the driver of the death car, nor give oath as to the license number, the factors described above, climaxed by the identification of the victim's hair on the fender of the automobile, convinced the jury of the guilt of the accused and he was convicted of manslaughter.

Sometimes it is a bit of fibre that unravels a crime mystery. It was a minute particle of silk that sealed the fate of Frank Nolan. Nolan was a neurotic who continually suspected his wife of unfaithfulness. This phobia brought death to his friend Samuel Waterbury.

Be that as it may, Nolan shot Waterbury, but claimed he had acted in self-defense. There seemed to be no way to disprove his statement.

After the shooting he notified the police. The officers listened to a stuttering story from the trembling lips of the husband.

"Waterbury came here this evening, shortly after my wife had gone to a picture show. I was tired and wanted to stay home." Nolan brushed back his unkempt hair as he tried to compose his shattered nerves. His torn and rumpled clothing and the disarranged room indicated that there had been a struggle before death had come to the victim.

Nolan shuddered as his eyes rested on the crumpled body that lay in a pool of blood in the center of the living room. "I knew he had come to see my wife, as he had done so often before. He was always annoying her with his attentions. I told him I wouldn't stand for it. I got pretty mad, I guess.

"Then he drew a gun. I jumped at him just as he fired, and the shot went wild. We wrestled, and finally I got the gun and shot him—the dirty hound!"

This story seemed to gibe with conditions as officers found them. Overturned furniture of the room testified to the life and death struggle. The bullet wounds in the victim's body were powder-burned, indicating that the shooting had been done at close range—during the struggle, perhaps. One bullet had pierced the ceiling—no doubt the bullet that had gone wild."

Examination of the gun showed that four shells had been fired, but only three shots had left a mark, two in the body of the deceased and the other in the ceiling.

The investigating officer got his first hunch that Nolan's story was not "all wool and a yard wide" when his wife returned from the cinema. Her hysterics on entering the room of death seemed not quite genuine; and when she fainted away, the detective noted the significant absence of the death pallor of face, lips, and even gums that invariably accompanies the true faint. He wondered if she weren't playing possum to avoid questioning.

The following day I was asked by the local chief of police to investigate the case. The missing bullet focused my curiosity. I thought it queer that no trace of it could be found at the scene of the crime. When all clues fail, it is always through the unknown element that the investigator hopes to unravel a mystery. It seemed unreasonable that in this case one shot more or less should make any material difference in the innocence or guilt of the principal in the case. And yet, I could not dismiss from my mind the unknown element of the missing bullet.

I questioned Mrs. Nolan, but to no purpose. She substantiated her husband's story that she had gone to a picture show before Waterbury had arrived at their home. Concerning her relations with the deceased she was very vague.

"Oh, yes," she declared, "Sammy has been a very dear friend, but Frank had no reason to be jealous. We were good friends, that's all." Her voice quavered, and her eyelids fluttered as though she were trying to conceal tears just beneath the surface.

Examining the room in which the shooting occurred, I began a systematic search for the missing bullet. There seemed to be nothing else that could throw light on the affair, and there seemed to be little hope in that direction.

Inch by inch, almost, I covered the walls and finally the floor. A small depression in the linoleum caught my attention. It might have been made by one of a hundred things, and yet that one thing might have been a bullet that had ricochetted. This mark was about three feet from the wall directly below a window. The path of the bullet would have been toward the wall. A casual glance revealed no mark. Closer examination revealed the mark of a bullet in the plastering underneath a torn bit of the wall paper. The frayed edges of the wall paper beneath the apron of the window casing had concealed the bullet mark. Carefully I extracted the bullet.

Under the microscope there was revealed a tiny strand of pink fibre adhering to the bullet. This fibre proved to be silk.

This bullet had passed through some pink silk clothing.

A new angle, perhaps. And still, it might mean nothing at all. It was possible that either Mr. Nolan or the deceased had worn some sort of pink silk clothing, an undergarment, shirt, or maybe a handkerchief. This was checked, and I found not a trace of clothing through which this bullet might have passed without affecting the story told by Mr. Nolan.

The only alternate hypothesis—a third party must have been present during the shooting. And very likely it had been a woman who wore a pink dress.

"What kind of clothing did Mrs. Nolan wear on the night of the killing?" I asked the chief of police.

"A brown suit of some sort. Didn't notice particularly. What of it?"

I told him about the silk fibre found on the bullet. We decided to search the Nolan home once more. In the wife's boudoir we found a pink silk petticoat. It was punctured with two holes that might have been made by a bullet. Also we found the brown tweed suit Mrs. Nolan had worn the evening of Waterbury's death. It too contained two tiny holes in the same relative position as the holes found in the petticoat.

A laboratory examination of the material in the petticoat revealed it to be identical in texture and color to the strand of silk found on the bullet.

Mrs. Nolan had lied to us! She had been an eyewitness to the shooting! She was shielding her husband.

We confronted the woman with this evidence, showing her the holes in the clothing. She renewed her hysterics, but we waited patiently for her cries and sobs to subside.

"He'll kill me! He'll kill me!" she screamed.

"Who will kill you?"

"Frank—if I tell!"

"Frank can't harm you now. He's safe at headquarters."

Bit by bit we wheedled the true story from the reluctant lips of the woman.

Waterbury had called on an informal visit to the Nolan home. The three had chatted for a few minutes when Nolan had left the room. He had returned directly, a virtual madman, wild with a jealous passion. Waving a gun, he had ordered Waterbury from his home. Then he had leveled the revolver directly at the unwelcome visitor. Mrs. Nolan had leapt in front of her friend to protect him. A reflex action prompted by a desire to protect his wife had caused Nolan to lower his gun as he pulled the trigger. The bullet had passed harmlessly through the wife's clothing, hit the floor and ricochetted into the wall.

Throwing his wife aside, the infuriated man had continued his murderous attack, but at that moment Waterbury had grappled with his assailant, causing the next bullet to pierce the ceiling. The hand-to-hand encounter had proved fatal to Waterbury. Two bullets had found their mark. Mrs. Nolan had fled to a cinema to avoid embarrassing questions.

Nolan verified this version of the shooting in a confession he made subsequently.

But for a tiny thread of silk, almost miraculously preserved at the tip of a bullet, Nolan might have escaped the arm of the law.

14

BLACK LIGHT: THE INVISIBLE DETECTIVE

One of the primary tools of the scientific criminologist is identification by comparison. This aspect of the detective laboratory has as many ramifications as there are peoples or substances in the whole wide world.

However striking this statement may be in its implication, it is fundamentally true. Sometimes the criminal investigator must determine minute differences between similar things or substances; at other times he must establish points of similarity between two or more things or substances. Then, again, he may seek an unknown factor by means of fixed standards. The ultimate purpose, of course, is to determine the relationship of a thing or substance to a particular crime or to a particular suspected criminal.

Boiled down to its essentials, this all involves identification by some sort of comparison. The diversity and magnitude of the task is best emphasized by the statement that no two things in the world are exactly alike in every particular. Like most general statements this has its exceptions; but it is true enough to be pertinent. Striking similarities, accompanied by minute differences, and glaring differences to the eye accompanied by a basic similarity, make the task the more difficult.

To this task of identification by comparison, science has brought its best skill. The microscope and the chemical test tube have played important roles.

Now science has brought another weapon against the criminal, more weird and uncanny in its results. It is the use of ultraviolet and infrared light rays, which are invisible to the naked eye and are designated by many writers as "black light." Sometimes its achievements may seem to be black magic. One may look directly into a powerful infrared lamp and see no light whatever; but photographs may be taken with the rays from such a lamp, in total darkness as far as the eye can perceive.

Dr. A. J. Pacini, director of the Pacini Laboratories, Chicago, has given a very interesting sidelight on its origin. He writes:

> Crime detection by ultraviolet light is the outgrowth of a secret unearthed in a snail's shell in the ancient city of Tyre. Snails pursuing their proverbial slow pace across the grounds of this maritime city of Phoenicia were found to secrete a whitish fluid which turned a rich violet color under exposure to a few hours of sunlight. A Phoenician with a business eye made the first royal purple and based the original dye industry upon his observation of this phenomenon.
>
> The principle involved was the fluorescence and the changing of certain substances under exposure to ultraviolet light which, in the case of the snail, came from the sun. Today the identification of materials by their peculiar fluorescences under ultraviolet rays offers an entirely new method of attack to the criminologist.[1]

Though many near-miracles in crime detection have been performed by means of the "black light," its technique is relatively little known, and its potentialities seem almost limitless. As experimentation and research continue, its uses will cover an ever-widening field.

The basic factor involved is the varying fluorescences of different substances when viewed under invisible light. Each type of matter that reacts to the ultraviolet light has its own peculiar fluorescent sheen or glow, with varying colors and varying shades of

---

[1] "The Ultraviolet Detective," *American Journal of Police Science*, May-June, 1930. Quoted by permission.

the same color. In my own laboratory and in the laboratories of Dr. Herman Goodman of New York City and Dr. Pacini of Chicago, a large number of substances have been made the subject of experiments, and their fluorescent qualities noted and catalogued.

As a result, when a criminologist with ultraviolet equipment is faced with an unknown substance, he places it under the powerful "black light" and there may recognize it by its characteristic fluorescence. Then he confirms its identity by other proven tests. Without the primary identification of the fluorescence he may not even guess what to look for. Ordinary chemical or physical tests may not only be futile, but may destroy the substance before any definite results have been obtained.

This fluorescent property of various substances has greatly aided the criminologist in his work of comparative identification. Take hair, for instance. Hair of two individuals may seem identical in color, texture, and structure, but seen under ultraviolet light, it often shows a marked variation in fluorescence. This may be caused by adherent matter, such as pomades, hair tonics, dyes, or bleaching matter. Sometimes the variation of fluorescence of hair may be caused by the habitual use of some sort of drug. One suspect was identified by a peculiar purplish fluorescence of the strands of hair found in a brush left behind in his hurried departure from a hotel room. It was the fluorescence of a drug. This drug through continued use had reached the hair of the suspect. Dr. Pacini has had a similar case.

Many interesting things have been learned about common objects. Leather tanned by one process has a different fluorescent glow from that of the same kind of leather tanned by a different process. The difference lies in the chemicals used in the tanning process. Ordinary window glass can often be identified as coming from a certain source. One piece of glass placed under invisible light may reveal fluorescent properties not possessed by another piece that otherwise looks identical.

By means of "black light," imitations can often be distinguished easily from the real thing. This is particularly true in the case of certain essential oils and precious stones. Exhaustive tests are now being made with "black light" to determine whether the different races of man can be distinguished by the fluorescence of teeth and bones. Some interesting differences have already been noted between the white, black, and yellow races. A direct application of this last method could have been made in a recent Florida case where a coroner's jury was unable to determine the race of a man whose body had been in the water for months.

Even more marvelous are the results obtained by the microscopist using ultraviolet light in the study of poisons and bacteria. With the fluorescence microscope he can detect the presence of microscopic crystals of certain poisons in amounts so small as to defy ordinary methods. If certain drugs are present, even in minute quantities, this is revealed by characteristic fluorescence.

In the field of forgery, questioned documents, secret writing with invisible inks, and so on, the ultraviolet ray has been an invaluable asset to the criminologist. Different kinds of inks fluoresce with different colors under invisible light beams. The same is true of certain special typewriter ribbons.

A questioned will was brought to me for examination. To the naked eye it was letter-perfect. There seemed to be no variations in the writing; no erasures were apparent. Placed under the ultraviolet light the document made a weird appearance. The paper itself took on the dark violet shade of the light to which it was exposed. Practically all of the typewritten matter disappeared, except a few letters that had been inserted by a typewriter with a different ribbon. These letters stared out starkly with a faint phosphorescent glow. Furthermore, it was evident that the name of the original beneficiary had been erased chemically, and another name superimposed.

By means of a special "V-ray" camera equipped with chemical filters contained in cells of pure fused quartz allowing the passage of only reflected invisible rays, it was possible to make a permanent photographic record of this forgery and expose it to the satisfaction of a court of law. The most skillful forger who attempts to alter documents is soon brought to justice when the "black light" and modern science are put on his trail.

Invisible writing, an ancient means of sending secret messages, is also detected by the ultraviolet beam. Under the purplish glow of this light many invisible ink writings can be read as easily as a printed page.

Startling as are the revelations of invisible light when applied to documents, the chance discovery of an unknown quantity incidental to an examination often proves more spectacular.

About the time I was conducting a study of precious stones as they appear when viewed with various combinations of filters and different wave bands of light, an incident occurred which clearly illustrates the possibility of many persons' wearing spurious gems which they believe to be genuine.

A wealthy woman client of mine was in the laboratory on the occasion of my demonstrating to her evidence of an erasure, an important bit of evidence in a lawsuit in which she was involved. During the demonstration her hand, on which she wore a ring set with five large stones, came under the strong rays of ultraviolet light as she took hold of the document. Four of the stones shone with a brilliant fluorescence which brought from the woman an exclamation of surprise and delight: "Oh, look how beautiful my diamonds shine under this light!" Then, she exclaimed, "But, look, one of them looks a dead purplish blue and has no lustre. It does not shine like the others."

From my study of diamonds under "black light" I had learned that very few diamonds fluoresce or appear at all brilliant under the ultraviolet light. It is only a few that appear with the peculiar luminescence. Out of some hundred genuine diamonds which I had examined, but three appeared with any degree of luminescence.

I asked her where she had purchased her ring, and she stated that it had been a gift from a very dear gentleman friend who had paid an exorbitant amount for it and she knew that it had been purchased from a reliable jeweler. The ring had never been out of her possession except for cleaning, and then only for a few moments while she waited for it.

I explained to her what my findings with diamonds had been, and naturally she was more than interested to know whether or not the stones in her ring were genuine or imitation.

The ring was submitted to three well-known reliable jewelers. One of them pronounced all of the five stones to be genuine, and one would not state his opinion without an extended examination. The third man, who had made a lifelong study of gems, pronounced the ring to have only one diamond, the other four being beautiful stones, but not diamonds.

Many gems considered genuine by their owners are in reality clever imitations or stones of a class and character different from what they are thought to be. Since the foregoing occurrence I have had many interesting experiences wherein even reputable jewelers have been fooled and have sold colored stones as genuine only to find out later that they themselves had been duped in their purchases.

The identification of precious stones involves more than a critical examination with a jeweler's glass.

There is a particular case in which the ultraviolet light played an imposing part in a court proceeding. I have never seen such an expression of bewilderment as was evident upon the face of a witness when he saw the positive proof developed by the silent evidence of the ultraviolet light.

The two Lawrence brothers had become interested in a growing lumber concern. This they bought, and Jerry, otherwise unoccupied, ran the business while Arthur, interested only in a financial way, occasionally advanced capital to the concern.

Suddenly, Jerry died, leaving a widow. The estate came up for probate, at which time Arthur learned that his sister-in-law, the widow, claimed the entire business and turned a deaf ear to his entreaties for a settlement. Stunned by this unexpected turn of affairs, Arthur placed a claim for his share. It was denied that he had any claim, and for this reason, he obtained a court order impounding the company books and requiring an examination of them.

The bookkeeper had now suddenly shown a more than friendly interest in Jerry's widow, and he became an important witness in the litigation. He also declared that Arthur was not known as a partner. Certain figures, writings, and erasures had attracted the attention of the plaintiff's attorney, who determined to bring to light every bit of evidence concerning the ledgers.

The legal contest began, and it soon became evident to the plaintiff's attorney that proper laboratory examination of the ledger sheets might bring out hitherto unexpected facts. During a three-day recess period over the week-end he obtained from the judge permission to have me make a laboratory examination of the ledger sheets with particular reference to the erasures contained therein.

I was able to complete my examination in time to return the books just before court opened. No one on the opposing side knew of the examination which had been made. The books had techni-cally been in the constant possession of a clerk of the court, who was present during the entire examination. The case was being tried in the court house of one of the smaller counties in the state of Washington. I had worked on previous matters with various county officials here, and for this reason the attorney who employed me requested that I remain in my car a half-block away from the court house while awaiting my call to the witness stand.

Previous to giving my testimony I did not know any of the facts concerning the case or the testimony of the bookkeeper, who was to testify this same morning. The following is taken from the court reporter's notes relating to the bookkeeper's testimony concern-ing the erasures in the books.

"You admit that you made these erasures found throughout the ledger?" queried the attorney.

"Yes."

"Why did you make them?"

"This was the manner in which we made corrections all the time."

"Did any of these erasures pertain to Arthur Lawrence in any way?"

"Absolutely not," he answered.

"Are you positive?"

"Yes."

"You realize you are under oath?"

"Certainly."

"'What appeared where these erasures are? What did you erase?"

"I do not remember."

"Your Honor, I wish permission to call another witness before continuing and finishing with this witness."

At this point I was called in, to the surprise of the opposing attorney with whom I had worked on previous matters. Qualification and direct examination followed immediately while the bookkeeper sat in the front row during my testimony.

"You have made an examination of the books in question, Mr. May?" I was asked.

"I have."

"Will you state what examination you made and what you found?"

"I find that there have been numerous erasures throughout the ledger which are very apparent. Even the erased figures are visible to the naked eye beneath new insertions. There are two erasures which are not apparent to the naked eye and over which there is no writing visible. I placed these ledger sheets beneath the ultraviolet light and find that in the original writing on page three, fourth line down from the top of the page in the first column of figures, there is a figure $5000 for which there is no explanatory note. Immediately beyond the last zero there appeared beneath the ultraviolet light the characters 'Rec'd of A. F. Lawrence.' I made photographs of what I observed under this light, for these characters were not visible in ordinary light.

"On page nine, the seventh line down from the top of the page and in the first column of figures, there appears a space in which I found the figures $2500.00. The period is plainly visible to the naked eye upon close examination. Evidence of the erasure is only visible under the ultraviolet ray here. To the left of this figure are found the characters 'Dp. A. F. L. —' indicating the figures $2500.00. These are shown in this photograph."

"You made these photographs yourself, Mr. May."

"Yes."

"That is all, Mr. May. Your witness," said the attorney.

"No cross-examination," answered the defense attorney, now apparently completely set back by the large photomicrographs, which he carefully examined himself.

The bookkeeper was recalled to the stand for further cross-examination and Arthur Lawrence's attorney began questioning.

"Do you understand the meaning of the oath that you have taken?"

"Yes," he answered with an apparent lump in his throat.

"Your Honor, I wish to have this witness sworn again. He was sworn in last Thursday, but not this morning."

"Very well," said the Court. "Swear the witness, Mr. Clerk."

After being sworn in again, the bookkeeper was asked if he understood the meaning of perjury.

"Yes," he answered in a tremulous voice. Beads of perspiration were visible on his brow. His cocksure air had now left him.

"Here are some photographs of the original writing which you admit erasing. You will note the words which have been brought back. Are they in your handwriting?"

"They look like it," he answered.

"Well, don't you know?"

"I can't be sure."

"Isn't it a matter of fact that the entries showing Arthur Lawrence's interest in the concern were written by you and erased by you?"

"They might have been. I can't remember."

"Well, no one else did any writing or erasing except you, did they?"

"No, I guess not."

"We are not interested in what you guess. Did you or did you not write the entries reproduced in these large pictures? Answer yes or no!" demanded the attorney.

Everyone in the court room was leaning forward to catch this answer, as the bookkeeper's voice was now barely audible. The court reporter, his pen poised, looked up, slightly turning his head toward the spectators while waiting for the answer. You could have heard a pin drop.

"Yes, I wrote them," finally came the faint response.

"What did you write?" pressed the attorney.

Slowly and with a cracking voice, he read the name of the dead brother and the amounts he had invested.

When the bookkeeper carefully erased the entries in the privacy of his locked office away from human eyes, he had not thought of the mute testimony of the "black light" which was to dishonor him in the court room more pitilessly and more impressively than any words of a human witness. Not only did he face a charge of perjury, but the widow, who evidently had used him merely as a tool and to whom he looked for assistance in his trouble, now ignored him and seemed utterly indifferent to his fate.

It has been my experience that regardless of the careful planning of the criminal, his caution, subterfuge, and elaborate efforts to conceal evidence of his crime, some event or circumstance entirely beyond his anticipation, knowledge, or control will ultimately bring him to an inglorious end.

While monochromatic light and different combinations of the separate parts of the spectrum are useful in the scientific detective laboratory for the detection and identification of physical clues in special cases, daylight still remains the greatest light source to the criminologist for the examination of material both in the field and in the laboratory.

Daylight, however, is not always available in the laboratory or in the field while examining the interior of premises at the theatre of the crime, and science has again come to the aid of the criminologist as well as of industry and commerce. The development of an actual artificial daylight lamp which for practical purposes equals the visible daylight spectrum, duplicating all of the elements of daylight, has now been achieved. It may be used for illuminating objects at the scene of a crime as well as for offering a constant source of portable daylight for microscopic and photographic work in the laboratory.

It has long been known by scientists that the spectrum of carbon dioxide was the one best suited for the comparison of color, and a new lamp utilizing the carbon dioxide spectrum has just been achieved in what is known as the "Seerite Lite." I have found the application of this new contribution of science to be almost unlimited in the scientific detective laboratory for the examining of fingerprints, comparing handwriting, precious stones, and textile fibres.

Many substances, colored objects, powder marks, inks, chemicals, and stains of various kinds require examination by daylight, and such inspections have to be deferred on account of nightfall; thereby valuable time is often lost during an investigation.

In the application of this new light to modern crime detection science has kept pace and in many cases has actually turned the criminal's night into day.

15
CURSED BY BLOOD

And [the Lord] said, What hast thou done? the voice of
thy brother's blood crieth unto me from the ground.

And now art thou cursed from the earth, which hath
opened her mouth to receive thy brother's blood from thy
hand;

When thou tillest the ground, it shall not henceforth
yield unto thee her strength; a fugitive and a vagabond shalt
thou be in the earth.

—Genesis 4:10-12

This biblical record of the first murder, when Cain slew his
brother Abel, with its terrifying blood curse, is not without paral-
lel in modern criminology.

The blood of a murder victim cries out for vengeance, and the
trained investigator, understanding the language it speaks, is usually able to track the killer by the trail of blood he leaves behind.
Truly the curse of blood is on the head of every murderer.

Throughout the ages human blood has been the subject of superstitious fears and dreads. There is something sinister about blood.
Even today many individuals cannot look upon it without a nau-
seous faintness. Were it not for the spilling of blood, murder would
not be nearly so gruesome as it often is. Also, the fate with which
the murderer is cursed would not be so inevitable.

Blood at the scene of a crime usually seals the fate of the murderer. The premeditative killer knows this and often uses the most

diabolical cunning in trying to erase the traces of blood. To the criminologist it is of the greatest importance as physical evidence in a homicide case, while it is also the most difficult trace for the criminal to eradicate from his person and from the scene of crime.

Most murderers are cursed by the blood of their victims. Try as they will, murderers can never foretell what may happen during the killing. It is not easy to commit murder. Life is a tenacious thing, and the dying individual seems to have superhuman strength to fight off his assailant.

In this struggle blood is spilled—on the murderer's hands, on his clothing, on furniture, and on floors. The assailant may leave his fingerprint in blood, and often does, for by its very nature, blood is an admirable medium for this purpose.

Bloodstains at the scene of a crime can tell a great many things. I have known them to tell whether or not the victim was killed in self-defense, whether or not death was instantaneous, whether it was murder or suicide. It often tells clearly the movements of the principals during the struggle, the position of the victim when murdered, whether sitting, standing, kneeling, or stooping.

Much has been learned by the study of bloodstains in their relation to a crime. Because this study is a very special phase of criminology, I have coined a word to designate its full significance. It is "Sanguilocologic," meaning blood, its location, and the logical conclusions drawn therefrom.

Perhaps, the most important aspect of reconstructing a crime by means of bloodstains is the nature or outline of the spatters, drops, and stains. For instance, a drop of blood with peculiar radiating spatters would indicate that the blood was from the lungs, the air bubbles in it causing a characteristic splash. A perfectly round drop of blood with a saw-tooth edge or sunburst effect indicates that the blood dripped from a stationary object from a given height. An elongated drop of blood, sometimes trailing to a fine hair, shows that the bleeding object was moving and in what direction.

This characteristic of a drop of blood proved the undoing of the fiendish murderer of a wealthy old man, who lived alone in his home. The assailant had entered by a window, shot and clubbed the man to death as he lay in bed. Death had been instantaneous, or practically so. The investigation disclosed a series of drops of blood on the floor of the room in which the murder was committed. Minute examination of these stains revealed the following facts: The blood was that of the assailant, for it would have been physically impossible for them to have come from the murder victim who lay in bed. Furthermore, the bloodstains told me that the assailant had gone to the front door, stopped there a minute or so, and then returned to the other end of the room. Also, that the assailant was wounded on the left side of his body, probably his left hand.

This latter fact was supported by blood found in an open cabinet drawer. The bloodstains on the floor showed distinct characteristics of movement. A series of elongated or elliptical stains led from the cabinet to the door. These were on the left, facing the door. At that point there were a number of circular drops of blood, showing that he had been standing still. On the right side facing the door were a number of stains that indicated movement in the opposite direction, showing that the man had turned around and walked back. He had cut his left hand while it had fumbled through a drawer containing some loose safety razor blades, no doubt looking for valuables. Then he had gone to the door, the top of which was of glass. He had stopped to see if the coast were clear, and probably a passing automobile had prompted him to turn around and retreat into the shadows of the room.

We were thus able to narrow the search to a man with a wounded left hand, with a cut from a sharp instrument. He was found and definitely identified as the murderer by the gun found in his possession.

Usually, however, it is the blood of the murder victim that forms the most incriminating evidence. If the assailant is spattered with his victim's blood, nothing much short of burning all his clothing will destroy this evidence. Ordinary washing is not entirely efficacious, for blood will often be detected in the linings of pockets, in seams of clothing, between the outer and inner soles of a shoe, and even under the finger nails or in the pores of the assailant's skin. Usually, in an effort to wash away all traces of the evidence of blood, the affected clothing is scrubbed in hot water rather than cold, so as to do a good job. The reverse procedure would be more effective, for hot water sets the color of blood and makes it the more difficult to remove. The curtilage, or ring around the bloodstain, is always visible if a bloody garment is washed in hot water. I have previously mentioned the shirt that had been boiled and still showed evidence of a large bloodstain when the suspect was photographed.

A Kennewick, Washington, woman had been murdered with an axe. Her husband was suspected. The murderer had washed the axe free of blood. (So he thought.) The axe was submitted to me along with other exhibits, and apparently the man had done a good job of laundering. However, when I took the axe apart from the handle, I found stains where the two had joined. And these stains were human blood. The husband was convicted.

Then there was the case of William R. Woodall, a Wenatchee man, who was murdered while chopping wood in his woodshed. He had been attacked from behind. His head was slashed and beaten, and his neck was broken. During the investigation it was thought that a large soup bone found in the yard had been the weapon used by the assailant. However, laboratory tests showed no traces of blood on the bone, but did reveal human blood on the axe and an automobile jack, thus determining the weapons of assault. Minute splatters of human blood were also found on a woman's dress, blouse, and shoes. The shape and size showed them to be from a wound as a blow was struck. The woman confessed and is now serving a life sentence.

Such cases as these could be quoted by the score. In following chapters I will relate in detail some of the more dramatic cases where bloodstains predominated in establishing guilt.

However self-evident bloodstains may be at the scene of a crime, they would often confuse and elude the observation of a layman. Blood does not always look like blood. Exposure to the sun, for instance, makes it appear gray instead of bright red. Or it may look like dye, oil, fruit juice, rust, paint, tar, or ink. This variation in color is caused by the age of the stain, the substance on which it is found, the temperature, and so on. These factors make blood assume every imaginable tint—reddish brown, greenish brown, light olive-green, light rose—and sometimes it becomes almost colorless. On colored cloth, for instance, it might require ultraviolet light to detect bloodstains.

The investigator takes great care to preserve a bit of blood at the scene of a crime. Sections of floors or walls have been removed to secure a bloodstain intact. Loose dirt containing blood is treated underneath to give it adherent qualities. If blood is on a rough substance that cannot be cut or scraped, it may be moistened and absorbed or lifted by filter paper.

Often a case hinges on the fact whether a bit of blood is of human or animal origin. Fortunately, if conditions are favorable, science can tell us infallibly whether questioned blood is human or not.

If the Patriarch Jacob had lived in this day and age he would not have been deceived by his sons when they bought him Joseph's gaily colored coat that had been dipped in the blood of a kid to convince the father that the boy had been killed by a wild animal.

It is comparatively simple to determine whether a stain is blood or not, but it requires more skill and knowledge to tell whether it is human or animal blood.

Science has devised a means known as the "precipitin" test. Blood of a healthy human is injected into the veins of rabbits or chickens to produce a blood determination serum. Many of these rabbits and fowls die immediately, being unable to survive the toxic properties of human blood. The ones that survive are carefully nursed for six to ten days. By that time some of them have developed a very strong reactive serum that will be an indicator of human blood. In other words, the immunizing element developed in the rabbit's blood is the factor that enables the expert to recognize human blood in a test. Not all rabbits or fowls will develop antiserums.

The same great care is taken in making this test that is taken in hospitals for major operations. Instruments are sterilized and then neutralized to acidity and alkalinity. Each slide and tube is washed three times in boiling distilled water, then with alcohol, and plugged with sterilized cotton. There can be no doubt; for the life or liberty of an accused man depends upon the result.

A very dilute solution of the blood which is to be tested for its human or animal origin is placed in solution in tiny glass tubes which are then filled up with an equal amount of the serum developed from the blood of rabbits. If the proper technique is followed and it is human blood, a thin precipitate ring will form where the two liquids meet. Great care and experience are required to properly interpret the reaction.

In other words, if the two solutions are separated with an albuminous line showing between them, the suspected blood is that of a human. If the two solutions show no line of demarcation the suspected blood is that of an animal. Carefully conducted tests with other known bloods are always run as controls to verify the results.

The blood of the anthropoid ape reacts somewhat like human blood, giving some credence to the Darwinian theory.

If the people of Jacob's time had been conversant with this technique, the whole history of the Israelites might have been different, and perhaps the course of civilization might have been changed. Today it is one of the most potent weapons used by the scientific criminologist to combat that antisocial element of society which seems to be bent on destroying what little civilization we have acquired through the ages.

The murderer is cursed by the blood of his victim as well as his own.

16
Betrayed by Blood

The "perfect crime" has not yet been discovered. The most cleverly conceived and executed plan goes awry in some one or more particulars.

He who would destroy life must combat life in all its aspects. Even nature seems to conspire against the lust for murder. Perhaps Providence so wills it.

In the case of the McClurg murder, a few sagebrush that had been growing on Little Freezeout Hill for long years contributed materially toward sending John McClurg, wife-murderer, to life imprisonment.

Let us reconstruct the crime as nearly as possible by evidence discovered later:

McClurg and his pretty twenty-year-old wife of only a few months were driving along the highway between Caldwell and Emmett, Idaho. The Ford coupé stopped. Before the young wife knew what had happened, her skull was crushed by blows from a blunt instrument—perhaps a hammer which was missing and never found. It was usually carried, with some pliers on top, back of the seat. Some time elapsed that was unaccounted for. Perhaps the assailant was mustering courage to finish his dastardly deed. Starting up again, the car was driven on toward Emmett. When the Ford coupé reached the top of Little Freezeout Hill, it stopped.

Turning the wheels toward a steep embankment, McClurg sent the automobile with his mortally wounded wife down the incline.

Under normal conditions a car would turn end over end as it made its crazy descent down the steep embankment. Not so this Ford coupé.

It staggered down, and just as it was about to topple over and completely wreck itself, it struck a large sagebrush. This impediment to its drunken progress righted it and swerved it diagonally. Again it was about to totter and roll side over side down the hill when it side-swiped another big bush. Straightening up, it continued on its four wheels in some miraculous fashion until the bottom was reached. It probably wouldn't happen again in a million times. Explain it if you will!

The point is that the car was not wrecked as McClurg had expected. The crushed skull of Marie McClurg could not be explained away by her wild ride down the declivity!

Some time later John McClurg appeared at a farmhouse about two miles from the tragedy. Wild and disheveled, bleeding from superficial wounds on his face, he made a piteous figure as he begged the farmer for help to save his wife from a burning automobile at the bottom of Little Freezeout Hill.

"I've crawled all the way here on my hands and knees," he wailed.

Whether the automobile had caught fire from an explosion as it reached the bottom of the hill, or whether it was deliberately fired by McClurg, is a matter of conjecture. However, all things indicated that when the murderer realized that his plan of simulating death in a wrecked car had failed, he saturated the car and the body with gasoline and set it on fire.

At any rate, when the farmer and McClurg arrived at the scene, only the cinders of the burned car remained and beside it the charred body of the victim.

One thing, however, the assailant overlooked. When the car careened madly down the hill, an upholstered seat cushion tumbled out. When Sheriff Merl Dillon and Prosecuting Attorney H. M. Haag found it, they discovered a large bloodstain on it. This was the first element that aroused suspicion in the minds of the authorities.

The blood of Marie McClurg betrayed her husband.

With their suspicions aroused the officers became more alert for evidences of foul play. It seemed odd that the body of the woman should have been burned so completely under the circumstances; that it should be found lying outside of the wrecked car in this charred condition. Investigation disclosed that McClurg had a short time previously taken out a $10,000 life insurance policy on his wife, with double indemnity for accidental death. And this had been done under false pretenses. In his application for the insurance policy he had claimed that he was worth $14,000 in cash, that he did not use liquor, and that his wife was not pregnant at the time of application. All these statements were proved to be false. McClurg had so little money that he passed bad checks; a few days earlier he had been released from jail after serving a sentence for drunkenness and disorderly conduct; examination of the body of the dead woman revealed her to have been pregnant several months. Of course, this invalidated the policy according to the rules of this company, but it also told officials that McClurg was not a trustworthy, responsible citizen.

These facts prompted an even more rigorous investigation of the circumstances surrounding the tragedy. I was engaged to assist in this work. Inspecting the scene of the crime, we found much incriminating evidence, despite the fact that the automobile and the body of the victim had been almost completely destroyed by the fire.

An interesting, though seemingly an irrelevant discovery was that of a number of buttons neatly piled under a sagebrush. Microscopic examination of strands of wool adhering to these buttons showed that they matched the fabric of McClurg's vest.

However, the most significant evidence uncovered in the investigation was a bloodstain on the seat cushion that had tumbled out of the hurtling car. It was a crescent-shaped stain of human blood, obviously caused by oozing or dripping from the back of the head of an individual sitting on the right-hand side of the car. From its size and shape this stain could have gotten there in no other way.

It suggested that the victim had worn clothing about the neck that had somewhat stopped the flow of blood down the back of the seat.

And there had been a considerable amount of blood! It had soaked thoroughly into the seat cover, the seat upholstery, and even the padding below it. Serological tests of a bit of charred clothing taken from the back of the neck showed it to be blood-soaked.

Marie McClurg had been wounded severely before her body had been almost completely consumed in flames!

This was further established by a complete examination of the burned remains of the deceased. The major portion of the woman's skull was missing. The nature of the fractured bones surrounding the gap indicated that the fracture had been made before death or before the bone had been burned. The breaks were very definite and the fractures were charred, denoting that the bone had been broken before the flames reached it.

Even more conclusive was the fact that on the inside of the occipital protuberance there was a large amount of dried blood with a great blood clot that must have been made before death. In other words, Marie McClurg's heart was beating for some little time after the rupture of the blood vessel allowing the blood to collect in the skull. The heart had to be pumping in order to force enough blood into the cavity to displace the parts of the brain that had to give way to entry of such a large amount of blood.

This skull fracture could not possibly have occurred as a result of the wreck, for the car had not once turned over. The evidence clearly showed that the woman had been hit and cut on the head with a large instrument wielded with sufficient force to crush in the rear of the skull and that there was sufficient blood from these wounds to soak up the clothing of the neck and flow onto the back of the seat above the clothing line of her neck. Furthermore, she would of necessity have had to remain in this one position for some considerable time in order to lose the amount of blood found.

Thus it was definitely proved that Marie McClurg had been wounded some time before the car plunged over the side of the road. From the time the car started its nose dive down the hill until it reached bottom and started to burn, only a few seconds would have elapsed. This period was not sufficient to allow this amount of blood to collect.

An examination of McClurg revealed some rather incriminating circumstances. His face wounds were very superficial scratches that appeared to have been made by finger nails—perhaps his own. Though he claimed that his hands had been in the fire, it was found that not even the hair on the back of his hands had been singed.

And the trousers on which he had "crawled on hands and knees" over two miles were certainly not in need of mending at the knees.

Everyone connected with the case (including the jury) was convinced that McClurg had committed cold-blooded murder, despite his elaborate efforts to cover up evidence of violence.

He had gambled with life—and lost! Instead of securing a twenty thousand dollar insurance indemnity, he drew a death sentence! He was sentenced to be hanged in Boise, Idaho, Friday, June the 13th, 1930. He appealed, but the Supreme Court denied him a new trial. However, the Governor commuted his sentence to life imprisonment.

17
BLOODSTAINS AND A FIR NEEDLE

Though Lombroso's theory of the criminal type as to features has been discredited by modern criminology, his views were surely vindicated in the case of Eddie Whitfield.

This human fiend bore all the facial stigmata of Lombroso's criminal type, including the small furtive eyes that glittered venomously. It is a favorite device of the fiction writer to introduce an ape-man as his diabolical villain, but in this case there is no need of fantasy to picture Eddie Whitfield as a human gorilla.

And the atrocious crime he committed prompts me to say that human perversion sometimes seems to sink below the level of dumb brutes.

One rainy evening when days were short, in the little town of Battleground, Clark County, Washington, little eleven-year-old Anna Nosko started home from school along a familiar trail. For several years she had tripped happily along that same wooded path, and every giant fir and every fern seemed to be an old friend.

It never occurred to the little girl, nor to her parents, that danger could possibly lurk in the friendly serenity of this peaceful country with its pastoral charm and beauty that must be seen before it can be fully appreciated. It seems a pity that when man has driven back the dangers of the wilderness in the march of civilization, he himself should present the greatest danger of all.

On this fateful night Anna Nosko did not arrive at her home at the usual hour. Frantic parents sounded an alarm. Sympathetic friends and neighbors began a hurried, feverish search. Through

the dark wild night that seemed to brood sinister tragedy, the posse
continued its hunt for little Anna Nosko. At home the tear-stained
face of the mother revealed the agony that tore her heart. Can anything be more terrible than the agonizing suspense of a mother
when her child is swallowed up in the unknown darkness of a forest?

A little bit of a girl's dress, caught on a barbed wire of a fence
along the trail, led the posse to the child's body. The throat had
been cut from ear to ear.

Sheriff Thompson of Clark County did some remarkably good
work on this case. After investigating the few known facts, he began working on the theory that the child had been attacked by a
degenerate and then murdered. There seemed no clue whatever to
the assailant at the scene of the crime. But he began his hunt for a
sexual degenerate who might be guilty.

In a case of this kind every likely individual is open to suspicion. Eddie Whitfield, who lived near the lonely road that the girl
invariably used in going to and from school, became the object of
Sheriff Thompson's scrutiny.

From what I have said about Whitfield it is little wonder that
Thompson's suspicion was aroused. On seeing the place in which
he lived with his brother, one might expect anything. The dilapi-
dated shack was littered with every conceivable kind of rubbish.
Dirt! Filth! Degeneracy! It literally screamed at the visitor. The
place had not been swept in seven long years! The bed was a litter
of vermin-infected rags. Pillowcases had been undisturbed for so
long that pillows were worn through two thicknesses of covering.
The place smelled like a cesspool.

Dirt and filth are usually handmaidens of degenerate crime.

Sheriff Thompson searched his man. When he discovered
bloodstains on his underclothing, the sheriff didn't stop at half-
measures. He searched him thoroughly.

A short time previously Sheriff Thompson, one of Washington's
most successful officers, had attended a police lecture course where
I had addressed the group on methods of search in this particular
type of case. Sheriff Thompson stripped the suspect, and when he
found a few bits of foreign substance on his genitals, he carefully

wrapped them in cigarette papers—the handiest available material for adequately preserving this evidence.

Whitfield protested the bloodstains on his clothing had been made by the blood of a butchered chicken and volubly declared his innocence.

Directly after this I was called to Vancouver, the county seat, to confer with Sheriff Thompson on the case. Of course, an autopsy was in order, and to aid in this we called in Dr. Benson, pathologist of the Medical School of the University of Oregon.

Painstaking examination revealed that Anna Nosko had been violated before her murder. But it revealed more! In the ordinary case an inquest is held only to determine the cause of death. With the throat completely severed there could be no question as to the cause of the little girl's death.

In ordinary cases this would be an established fact and would be left at that. However, in scientific criminology nothing is taken for granted, and although a wound may appear to be mortal on the surface, the trained examiner will search further to discover all contributing causes or possibly another cause of death separate and apart from that which is found to be apparent.

Proceeding with the examination, we observed a slight abrasion back of the right ear, which at first seemed very insignificant; but a further examination of the skull revealed a fracture of the temple bone on the inner table of the skull. A piece of bone an inch square had been forced inward at right angles, causing a hemorrhage in the brain. There was a considerable blood clot, indicating that the girl had lived a considerable time after she had been hit on the head, and before her throat had been cut.

This supported the theory that Anna Nosko's assailant had been known to her. Because he had feared exposure, he had killed the girl after his brutal assault.

Even an internal blood clot has a story to tell! What type of weapon would leave so little evidence on the side of her head and still fracture the skull as before mentioned?

Inch by inch, Dr. Benson and I searched the body of the little girl. A mental picture had already formed in my mind as to how the crime was committed. There was a temporary pause in our procedure. We had made a careful examination of all of the organs with no striking developments. However, as the mental picture formed in my mind, I spoke of it to Dr. Benson: that there must be something that we had overlooked so far, for in all crimes of this nature there is always some telltale clue left which assists in identifying the perpetrator. I thought, with a strong magnifier, a more careful examination of the little girl and the preservation of all foreign substance which may have come in contact with the criminal during the commission of his act might be of value.

The thought was the father of the deed. At the mouth of the little womb we found what appeared to be a speck of dirt. At least it was foreign matter. This had been overlooked in our first examination. We carefully preserved this tiny bit of matter, and when viewed through the giant Revelarascope in the laboratory it proved to be the minute tip of a fir needle.

Serological tests of the stains on clothing worn by Whitfield at the time he was searched, and which he declared to be those of chicken blood, proved to be human bloodstains.

The net was tightening about the man.

But the small fragments of fir needles so carefully preserved by Sheriff Thompson—evidence that would have been overlooked by many officers—proved to be the final link that fastened this atrocious crime on Whitfield.

Examining under a powerful microscope the fir needles found on his person, I found that one of the needles had been broken at the tip. By placing the fir needle tip found near the girl's womb in juxtaposition with that of the broken fir needle found on the person of Whitfield, under a comparison microscope, it was readily determined that the two pieces had originally been one.

The ragged edges of the broken ends matched identically, in the same way as would the edges of two pieces of torn paper when fitted together.

The criminal, indeed, has reason to fear the marvels of science in the modern criminological laboratory.

When the jury a month later saw the photomicrographs of the two sections of the fir needle and saw how perfectly the broken edges matched—one found in the womb of the victim and the other on the assailant's genitals, the men needed little more evidence to bring in a verdict of "Guilty." He was executed at Walla Walla.

Nature through a tree had furnished the damning circumstance, the organ of human reproduction had held it so fast that it could be found to doom its violator. The vile-smelling Whitfield shack near the lonely road of Battleground is no more, for a mysterious fire burned it to the ground. Not a neighbor would stir a hand to extinguish the flames!

18
The Unknown Quantity X

It is always the unknown quantity x in the criminal investigation that baffles the officer of the law and makes a crime a mystery to stir the public pulse.

And this unknown element must be determined as accurately and surely as in any algebraic formula. However, the mathematician has an easier job than the criminologist. In an algebraic formula all factors are definite and correlated, whether of space, pressure, area, or weight. In a criminal case x may be any one of a number of things—a letter, a check, a weapon, a wound, a bloodstain, or a combination of all these factors.

The successful criminal investigator discovers the knowable factors and then develops the unknown quantity x by a process of deduction. To have a preconceived theory of a case before all the factors are known may be a stumbling-block in the solution of a crime mystery.

In determining the quantity x in a case of violent death bloodstains often play an important role. Sometimes it seems almost uncanny what bloodstains can tell the trained investigator.

When Thomas Cavanagh disappeared from his ranch near Cambridge, Idaho, and there was talk of murder, Jim Elliott, a brother-in-law, came under suspicion because he had allegedly made a threatening remark a short time previously. Had this lead been followed to the exclusion of all others, the real culprit might have escaped detection.

Instead of being guided solely by rumors and hearsay, I began my investigations at the scene of the crime to determine what the physical facts in the case would reveal.

Incidentally, when an investigator begins to look for evidence in a murder case, he does not observe things merely from the normal, eye-level perspective. He also gets the bird's view from above, the ant's view from below—views from every angle. It is surprising how different and more revealing a thing may appear under this scrutiny.

What I saw in Thomas Cavanagh's log cabin where he had been brutally murdered enabled me to reconstruct the whole crime.

In the corner of the cabin was a cook-stove, and near it a table. Going over the premises thoroughly, I discovered evidence of blood on the inside of the oven door; also on the inside of the oven. A portion of the bullet that had passed through the victim's head, entering the base of the skull and making its exit through the eye, was also found melted in the oven.

Under the table were some elongated drops of blood that revealed from what direction the blood spatters had come. Removing the oilcloth table cover, I discovered two distinct drops of blood, also elliptical in shape—one stain on the table top and the other on the back of the oilcloth. This indicated that the table cover had been folded back at the time of the crime.

Furthermore, these stains told me almost exactly the place and position and height of the man's head at the time he was shot from the rear. The location, size, and shape of these bloodstains indicated that they had come from a position almost level with the table top. Tracing back the lines of flight of these blood spatters along their axis developed a figurative triangle whose apex had been the head of the deceased, showing its position between the stove and the table and its relative distance from each.

From these factors it was possible to begin a reconstruction of the crime. Thomas Cavanagh had been kneeling in front of his stove, in the act of either putting something into the oven or taking it out, at the time he was shot.

This explained the unusual angle of the bullet through the victim's head, as though he had been shot from below. By visualizing the path of the bullet, taking into consideration the position of the man and the angle of the wound, it was found that the shot had come from a bed at the opposite side of the room and from about the level of a man sitting on this bed.

These factors of physical evidence gave us a very important clue to the perpetrator. He had been a visiting friend of the deceased, a man whom the victim had had no reason to fear.

Bloodstains on the wall of the cabin enabled us to trace the actions of the murderer further. These stains came from above and had been made by blood dripping from the ceiling.

Of course, all these bloodstains were tested biologically and established as human blood.

The stains on the wall prompted an investigation of the attic or loft of the cabin, which was entered through a small trapdoor in the ceiling. Human bloodstains were also evident in this loft. Obviously, the murderer had placed the corpse in the loft before permanently disposing of it, and the blood had dripped down on the wall.

All these factors were later verified and contributed a great deal toward securing a confession from the murderer. Developing the unknown quantity x in a crime is usually very disconcerting to a suspect. To him it seems weird and uncanny that almost every action at the scene of the crime is accurately reconstructed, and when faced with the facts, he not only is nonplussed but assumes that the investigator knows the whole story. His natural reaction is to admit it all in a confession.

Thus it was with Sam Hanna, who had murdered his cousin, Thomas Cavanagh. Suspicion was first directed toward Hanna when it was learned he had forged checks on Cavanagh directly after the latter's disappearance from his ranch.

When Jim Elliott, who had been arrested on suspicion, related how he had visited the Cavanagh cabin, and there had found Hanna ostensibly in charge of the place during the alleged absence of his cousin on a trip, suspicion began to revert. Elliott told how he had gone into the loft to get some oats for Cavanagh's horse, and there had placed his hand on what he thought was a "slick-ear," a butchered calf usually stolen from the range.

Elliott mentioned the "calf" in the attic when he came down, and Hanna admitted having killed a calf and cached it in the garret.

However, from what we had learned during our examination of the premises, we knew that the alleged calf had been the body of Thomas Cavanagh, placed there by Hanna. When arrested and confronted with the evidence we had uncovered, Hanna verified our findings and confessed the crime.

After placing the body of his victim in the loft, he left the place and went to the town of Weiser, where he forged checks on his victim's bank account. Later he returned to the Cavanagh cabin, removed the body, and packed it four miles during the dead of night to his father's ranch four miles away. There he buried it. But the blood of his victim that was left in the cabin he could not bury. It remained to point an accusing finger at the murderer!

Bloodstains, or rather an apparent lack of them, played an odd role in a recent suicide. A man was killed by a dynamite explosion. The scene of the tragedy was a little log cabin in the mountains of western Washington, where the deceased lived with another man. This friend told officials an almost unbelievable story; in fact, his story was discredited.

He claimed to have had no knowledge of the dynamiting until after it had occurred, though he had been in the small room at the time. The explosion had torn the man's torso almost to bits, and obviously the room was spattered with blood. The survivor maintained that he had been sleeping in the bed on which the body of the death victim was found at the time of the explosion, and knew nothing whatever about it until the explosion occurred.

This in itself seemed incredible to the authorities—that a man so near a violent explosion should have escaped without a scratch. Furthermore, there seemed to be not a single bloodstain on the survivor's person, though the room and its crude fixtures were literally covered with blood.

Naturally, the officials questioned his story. It seemed highly improbable that the man could have been in the cabin during the explosion. If he were lying about it, there must be an ulterior motive.

However, I questioned the man closely, and he related that he usually slept with the covers over his face during the early part of the evening because of the chill nights of the mountain climate. He protested that he had been sound asleep when the dynamite bomb exploded and was awakened to find the mangled body of his friend across him on the bed.

The investigator must often use his ingenuity to prove a man's innocence as well as his guilt. So it was in this case. It occurred to me that if the man were telling the truth, his story might be verified by examining the man's hair for traces of blood. Under the conditions he outlined, only his hair would have been exposed to blood spatters.

Carefully I combed his hair above a table covered with a large sheet of paper. Though the man had combed his hair several times since the tragedy, I still found a considerable amount of human blood in the combings. He had told the truth.

The victim, who had retired late, presumably had held the dynamite bomb as he sat on the side of the bed. His body had received the full force of the explosion, and thus protected his friend sleeping in bed beside him.

An examination of the blast victim's brain disclosed a lesion which accounted for his melancholy and suicide.

The case of Everett F. Lindsay, charged with wife murder, offers a vivid example of how bloodstains aid the criminologist in reconstructing crimes of violence.

On Easter morning, 1930, when thousands of Seattle people arose at dawn to participate in Sunrise Service, Lindsay, conscience-stricken by one of the most atrocious crimes in the history of the Pacific Northwest, arose with them. But not to worship! Like a thief in the night he stole out of the city with his foster daughter, Pearl, and fled to escape the consequences of his crime.

The murder of Audrey Lindsay, his wife, was not discovered until a few days later, when he was scheduled to appear before a secret tribunal of his lodge to account for the mysterious disappearance of his wife, who had been missing for about a week.

Lindsay did not appear, and an investigation was started by the prosecuting attorney of King County.

With consummate cunning the alleged murderer had covered his tracks, but the eyes of the law see the seemingly unseeable. It must be evident to readers of this volume that crime is the most hazardous of all vocations. The cunning of the arch criminal is of little more avail against the forces of the law than the blundering behavior of the amateur who commits a crime of passion.

Lindsay was designated an arch criminal. Meticulously he had tried to efface the evidence of the brutal killing of his wife. The corpse he had buried in an ingenious manner, and to the casual observer, the room in which the murder was committed had been placed in perfect order. Lindsay had viewed his work of effacement from the normal perspective and found it very satisfactory. But when the ant's view, the bird's view, and the penetrating eye of the microscope are brought to play on the scene of a crime an eloquent story of violence is usually revealed.

When officers began a systematic search of the Lindsay premises in West Seattle, they found some freshly turned earth in the back yard. Digging into this as a possible hiding place of the corpse, officers found some slightly buried garbage, old cans, and refuse. This seemed innocent enough, but a deputy sheriff pushed his spade beneath the garbage and inadvertently turned up a fresh green sprig. The earth below had recently been filled in!

It is often such insignificant little things that betray the most cleverly conceived plot.

Further digging revealed a sewer pipe—another blind that the murderer had put into the grave. Finally the body of the dead woman was recovered.

When I examined the home, I found that the murder had been committed in Mrs. Lindsay's bedroom.

Bloodstains told a complete story of what had happened! And yet, careful efforts had been made to efface them.

On the wallpaper at the side and at the head of the bed I discovered bloodstains, some as tiny as a fly speck. The location and shape of these stains revealed that the victim had been attacked while lying on the bed, perhaps asleep.

But that was not all. Blood spatters found under the front of the bed and at the base of an adjacent chiffonier indicated they had come from the region of the floor. The cruel ferocity of the murderer was plainly evident. After attacking his victim in bed, he had dragged her to the floor and there continued his blows with a heavy blunt instrument. The nature of the weapon was determined by examination and measurement of the wounds on the head of the deceased.

Other stains were found on the wall opposite the bed. The nature of these might have puzzled the uninitiated. They came from the region of the ceiling, and one spatter had fallen on the glass of a wall picture showing a charming domestic scene of wife, husband, and child before a fireplace. It was titled "Home Sweet Home"! Irony of ironies!

These bloodstains coming from above could be easily explained in the crime reconstruction. As the killer swung his heavy instrument, the adhering blood had taken flight ceilingward with each upward stroke, had formed a trajectory arc, and had struck the wall and picture on its descent.

Under the frame of the bed and on the floor under the bed I found definite smears of blood such as would be made by the movement of a bloody object. This could mean only one thing. After killing his victim by blows, first while she was on the bed and later on the floor, the murderer had pushed the body under the bed, where it remained until buried in the back yard.

This evidence showed the savage cruelty and ferocity of the murderer.

The crime was first directly linked to Lindsay when we found a shirt in his home with his laundry mark, which bore evidence of human bloodstains. This was further strengthened when I found a leather tie-holder in the room of the apartment house to which Lindsay and his foster daughter moved directly after the killing. This, no doubt, had been hanging on the wall of the bedroom, and when Lindsay removed it he failed to notice the tiny traces of blood.

Local officers discovered many another bit of contributing evidence that substantiated what we had already learned and gave additional information on the movements of Lindsay.

Another foster daughter, Helen, he had sent back to her parents before his Easter morning flight. Then began an intense manhunt for the alleged murderer. This was not easy, for he had had several days' start on the authorities. First trace of him was found in Oakland, California, where he registered at a lodging house as "Jack Grant" and daughter. There he deserted the child and fled. From this girl and the foster daughter in Seattle authorities got a very complete story of the crime.

For a year and a half Lindsay's whereabouts were unknown to authorities. He was apprehended and brought by airplane to Seattle from Los Angeles to face a first-degree murder charge. A youth in Los Angeles, seeing Lindsay's picture in a true detective story magazine, had recognized and reported him to the police.

19
Forgery and Crime

To the layman forgery may seem a minor crime, merely the illegal acquisition of money or property through the falsification of some sort of document—check, will, mortgage, or receipt. Even this aspect of forgery represents a tremendous drain on the social order, aggregating millions of dollars annually. Yet, of greater concern is the fact that a large percentage of forgers are also murderers.

The victim of forgery is often murdered as a precaution of the criminal against being found out in the minor crime. So it was in the Cavanagh case discussed in the previous chapter. So it is in many others. Crime is usually like a snowslide on a mountain: it may begin with a slight loosening of the snow in a small crevasse near the peak, but when the slide reaches the valley it becomes a terrifying avalanche of destruction.

Thus forgery has become a major concern of the criminologist, and he has used every known means to perfect methods of detection. Perhaps no branch of criminology has demanded more intense study and research than handwriting and its many ramifications. In this volume we cannot go into the technical details of the handwriting expert, and will merely give the high lights of the part he plays in crime detection and prevention.

Forgery is as old as civilization. Before the sciences of chemistry and physics were brought to bear on the forger, his chances of escaping detection were fairly good. Fifty or a hundred years ago the criminologist had to depend largely on his powers of observation and deduction in detecting the human element of error in a forgery. Though the master forger of today has acquired greater technique than his predecessor, he cannot hope to match his wit and skill with the modern scientific detective laboratory.

Even the most clever of forgers of ancient times made stupid errors that were discovered by the primitive methods of those days. Hans Gross, professor of criminology in the University of Prague, relates some interesting cases in this connection.[1] A master forger had created a document that was considered a work of art. But he made the mistake of referring in the document to "the late Majesty Francis," although the document was dated two years before the death of this emperor! A habit of speech had tricked him!

Another related case was that of Alexander Humphreys, who attempted in the High Court of Judiciary, Edinburgh, in the year 1839 to procure a large sum of money by introducing some allegedly ancient documents. These documents were marvelously executed, but it was discovered that one of them, dated 7th December, 1639, had been signed by the chancellor Archbishop Spottiswood, a worthy gentleman who had died during the preceding month, November, 1639.[2]

A letter allegedly written by President Garfield was first suspected of being a forgery because of the misspellings— "ecomony," "companys," "religiously."

Errors of the same type are committed by the forger today, but science has made the criminologist less dependent on that sort of detection. Today, it is relatively simple to detect the origin and age of inks and papers; what typewriter a manuscript was written on; erasures, which, whether chemical or physical, stand out like sore thumbs when viewed under "black light."

Even a good camera tells an interesting story of forgery in many cases. It operates on a manuscript in the same way that it often does on a human face. A woman may seem to have a perfect complexion, without a visible trace of a freckle. Yet, when she is

---

[1] *Criminal Investigations* by Hans G. A. Gross.

[2] *Essay on the Principles of Circumstantial Evidence,* by William Wills.

photographed any number of freckles may appear in the picture, which must be laboriously removed by the retoucher.

The reason for this apparent enigma is quite simple. The freckles, though invisible to the naked eye, do not reflect the light as do other parts of the face, and the sensitive plate of the camera records this fact. In the same way the altered portions of a document may defy detection by the naked eye, but the camera sees more on account of this variation of reflection either because of erasure or because of the use of different ink from the original.

No one can exactly duplicate the writing of another, for the habits of a lifetime cannot be acquired in a moment. Little idiosyncrasies of writing are invariably overlooked by the forger, and through this the falsification is usually detected.

So it was in the case of James E. Mahoney, forger and wife-murderer, a typical case of dual crime—a major crime to hide a minor offense. If Mahoney had not been an "ex-con" who had done a "stretch" for a cruel assault, he might have gotten away with it. And without the forgery, murder might not have been suspected.

The practice of police in checking the activities of known criminals was responsible for the first suspicion of crime. This routine procedure revealed Mahoney's possession of several thousand dollars' worth of diamonds. Police knew this spelled "heavy dough," and he was brought to Seattle police headquarters for questioning.

Then they learned that Mahoney had, a few weeks earlier, married a wealthy widow about twice his age—and Mahoney was thirty-eight. The jewelry, he claimed, belonged to his wife, and she had left it in his care while she made a trip to Havana.

He further related how he had accompanied his wife as far as St. Louis, and then Mrs. Mahoney had gone on the Cuba trip with a Mrs. Atkinson, leaving Mahoney to return home alone.

In support of this, Mahoney produced letters which his wife had written in the East, and travelers' checks bearing her signature. Triumphantly he produced a document in which his aged wife had transferred to him power of attorney over her entire fortune, including real estate. This latter he had already begun to dispose of.

To the average person, these proofs would have been conclusive evidence that everything was all right. But police decided that the story sounded queer. It was too perfect; too tailor-made. Mahoney was thrown into jail until further investigations could be made.

Inquiry among Mrs. Mahoney's friends revealed that the woman was inordinately fond of her diamonds, and that one of the rings found in possession of the husband, she had never been known to take off. It was also learned that Mahoney had complained that his wife was miserly with her money and would give him little more than pocket money.

In view of these developments it seemed highly improbable to Chief of Detectives Charles Tennant, of the Seattle Police Department, that Mrs. Mahoney had entrusted her husband with a fortune in jewels and had given him a power of attorney.

These suspicions were found to be well grounded when the questioned documents were examined in my laboratory and proved forgeries.

Several things about these documents testified to forgery. In the first place, it would have been impossible for anyone to write the signatures on the traveler's checks if the pen writing them was held in the hand as Mrs. Mahoney was in the habit of doing.

Furthermore, it would have been physically impossible for Mrs. Mahoney to write the forged signatures, for the writing showed a skill greater than that of Mrs. Mahoney. No one can write better than his best, and the writing in the forgeries was consistently better than the best writing of Mrs. Mahoney, though the latter's writing was cleverly simulated.

There was a decided wavering of lines in Mrs. Mahoney's writing, but there was no evidence of the exaggerated tremor that had made itself evident in the forger's attempt to simulate this wavering. This wavering of the pen had been overdone, with a tremulous hesitating and drawing movement entirely absent in the genuine writing.

Another characteristic of the genuine writing was a capital *S* that at first sight was not unusual, but when closely studied under the microscope was found to be peculiar and distinctive of Mrs. Mahoney's writing. This letter was used several times in the forged checks in giving the address, but in no instance did it have the little peculiarity always found in the genuine writing. It is the little, apparently inconsequential things that the forger always overlooks.

Other aspects of the writing were pertinent. The connecting stroke between *n* and *e* in the name Mahoney, as written in the genuine signature, was regular and curved; in the forged, it was irregular and angular. In the small letter *r* in "Mrs.," the genuine writing showed a tick at the top of the letter. This was consistently missing in the forgery. The letter *s* always ended upward in the genuine and downward in the forgery. The central loop in the capital letter *E* was always contracted in the genuine, always open in the forgeries.

It is by such minute variations that the handwriting expert establishes forgery.

But where was Mrs. Mahoney? This question became paramount in the investigation. She was last seen in her apartment on April 16, and it was on April 18 that Mahoney claimed he had accompanied his wife to the East.

It was on April 16 that Mahoney and a woman whom he introduced as his wife had made out a power of attorney and signed it in the office of a Seattle notary, E. J. Brandt. From a description of this woman, it was believed that she was Mrs. Dolores Johnson, sister of Mahoney.

But even more startling developments occurred. Police found an expressman who testified that on the evening of April 16 he had been called to Mahoney's apartment to move a trunk. Mahoney assisted in the work of loading it on to the vehicle and accompanied the expressman to the shore of Lake Union, where it was placed in a small rowboat. The expressman saw Mahoney row off on the dark waters with this baggage.

The police also found E. K. Boyd, a hardware merchant, who reported that Mahoney had purchased five pounds of unslaked lime and thirty feet of rope at his store on April 16. The net of evidence was closing in on Mahoney, but only the recovery of the body could definitely prove murder in a court of law.

It seemed evident that Mrs. Mahoney had been killed on April 16, her body placed in a trunk, covered with quicklime, and the trunk dumped into Lake Union.

Day after day, week after week, Lake Union and Lake Washington Canal, leading into it, were dragged and the body sought by divers. Nothing was found. Weeks dragged into months. Spring passed and summer came. Still nothing happened. Officers clung to the dragging job with amazing persistency.

It was disheartening, but in the end the submarine drag struck something—tore it loose—and a trunk bobbed to the surface! In it was the body of Mrs. Mahoney, identified by the peculiar bridgework of her teeth and by her clothing.

Mahoney went to trial for first-degree murder, and one of the strongest links of evidence against him was the established forgery of the power of attorney, the letters, and the signatures on the traveler's checks. Mahoney was convicted and went to his death on the gallows at Walla Walla, and Mrs. Johnson, his sister, who had actually done the forging, was convicted and sentenced to a term in prison.

20
The Kommerli Case

The forger, like all criminals, gambles with so many unknown factors that the odds are heavily against him. To win is an accident; to lose eventually, inevitable.

However skilful a forger's technique may be in imitating another's writing, he is still confronted with other factors that may trip up his schemes. The differences of papers and inks, the peculiarities of a particular typewriter, the variations in the shop that prints legal forms (often used in forgery) are just a few of the incalculable elements that often arise to embarrass and confuse the forger.

So it was in the Kommerli will case. It is not always possible to establish forgery definitely and positively merely by analyzing handwriting. Handwriting itself is a variable factor that may puzzle the expert. As a result, he may often need to support his opinions with other incriminating evidence found in the document.

A purported will and testament of Fred Kommerli, Seattle tailor, was one of the cleverest forgeries I have ever seen. And yet, even in this document, the absence of characteristic peculiarities of the writing of the deceased prompted the trial judge to state in his opinion that "it is impossible that the deceased should have changed the habits of a lifetime in the writing of this signature on the disputed will." And this despite the testimony of two so-called handwriting experts, one a bank cashier, that the questioned signature was genuine.

However, it was contributory evidence of the most surprising nature that supported my contention that the contested will was a forgery.

Fred Kommerli, an emigrant from Switzerland, had amassed a modest fortune of about $30,000. As is often the case, it became a subject of dispute among the heirs. It is rather a long story, but I will present only the facts pertinent to the case.

Kommerli came to the United States as a youth and later married and set up business in Illinois as a tailor. Later he moved to St. Louis, and there, when the only child, a daughter, was ten years old the couple were divorced. The wife retained the custody of the daughter. Two years later both parties were remarried.

Kommerli moved to California and later to Seattle, where he maintained a home until his death in the early part of 1929. His second wife had died years earlier. During his last years the man had made several wills, one which, in 1927, left one-half of the estate to his daughter, who lived in St. Louis, and divided the balance among named nieces and nephews in this country and in Switzerland.

However, a later will, dated February 23, 1928, was found in Kommerli's safety deposit box, naming Fred Broesser, Swiss Consul, as his executor. In this will the daughter was to receive only a small fraction of the estate, which was to be divided among twelve relatives.

This will was executed and was admitted to probate in the Superior Court of King County, Washington.

A month later the daughter arrived in Seattle from St. Louis. She visited and cultivated the acquaintance of a Mr. and Mrs. Shaylor, who were purchasing real estate from the Kommerli estate on contract. It seemed that she won the sympathy of these people because of the alleged unfairness of her father toward her in his will.

On this visit to Seattle the daughter secured possession of two suitcases containing the personal effects of her father after the contents had been thoroughly searched by the executor and an assistant. A previous search of these suitcases by a nephew of the deceased had brought to light the will of 1927, previously referred to, from which the signature had been cut.

When the daughter returned to St. Louis, she took these suitcases with her.

A short time later the executor received a telegram from the daughter, which reported the remarkable discovery of another will. This document, dated August 8, 1928, was allegedly found in a large, sealed envelope, concealed in a laundry folder of a shirt that had been laundered in Seattle, and which belonged to Kommerli.

The circumstances of this discovery were odd, to say the least. The finder declared that she had intended giving this shirt to the husband of a neighbor lady and had opened the laundry folder in the presence of this woman and her daughter when the envelope dropped out.

This will, witnessed by Mr. and Mrs. Shaylor of Seattle, was admitted to probate and purported to leave the entire Kommerli estate to the daughter, with the exception of a $500 bequest to an aged sister of the testator in Switzerland, who was blind.

Within six months other heirs under the first will instituted a contest against the will discovered in St. Louis.

Besides the striking coincidence of its discovery among clothes that previously had been searched by a nephew of Kommerli and in the executor's office, there was another circumstance that seemed unreasonable and which brought suspicion on its authenticity. Though the daughter had visited the Shaylors for some time and had had correspondence with them, they had made no mention of having witnessed a will by Kommerli a few months earlier!

The law firm representing the contesting heirs called me into the case as consultant. The first step was to determine, if possible, the authenticity or fraudulency of the signature.

After a thorough comparison of the questioned signature with a large number of Kommerli's signatures that were known to be genuine, I determined to my own satisfaction with mathematical certainty that the latest will was a forgery.

As previously mentioned, two other experts disagreed with me and pronounced the signature genuine. Another, while later agreeing that it was a forgery, assisted opposing counsel in cross-examining me at length, evidently for the purpose of befogging the issue if possible. However, the scientific analysis of this signature illustrated by means of large photomicrographs convinced the trial judge that the questioned document was a forgery.

However, this did not conclude the case of the contestants. Even more convincing were a few facts we learned about the legal form used for the will discovered in a shirt.

In the first place we learned that it had been printed by Lowman & Hanford, a Seattle firm, and was a stock blank that was sold throughout the Northwest. Also the legal form used by the former will was of this origin. The forger had been very adroit in this respect.

Further contributory evidence was a bombshell to the defense. I was able to prove conclusively that though the questioned will was dated August 8, 1928, the legal form on which it was written had not been printed until seven days later, August 15.

It is just such an inconceivable factor that upsets the carefully laid plans of most criminals.

In this case it was the slight variation in the printing process that was not foreseen and calculated by the forger. This printing firm makes a practice of letting its legal forms remain in type. New blanks are printed from time to time as required by the demand of the trade, the same type form being used in each instance.

This might seem to make it extremely difficult to determine from what particular "run" a will form originated. Yet an examination of specimens of these legal forms, printed from the same form, but at different times, showed marked differences which were hardly apparent except under close scrutiny. For instance, the placement of the type form in the press and its tightening by the printer might develop a variation between different printings.

In this case, examination under the microscope of the contested will and a specimen of a similar form printed on August 15 showed identical defects of type, defects that had been caused by the wear and tear of printing and by handling during the "make-ready." Earlier printings showed no evidence of such defects.

This evidence was not conclusive, however, for there was the possibility that these defects in letters had developed during the latter part of the previous printing of August 6, 1927. I, therefore, sought other identifying clues that would positively identify the particular printing of August 15, 1928, and differentiate it from any other as shown by the samples kept on file by the printing firm.

This identifying evidence I found in a variation of spacing between two lines of the legal form, caused, no doubt, by the addition of a thin slug line when the form was locked in the printing press. This slight variation of printing definitely established the fact that the form used in the contested will had been printed on August 15, though it was purported to have been made as much as seven days earlier.

When this evidence was produced, one of the experts who had been so diligently assisting the opposing counsel trying to discredit my conclusions was not called, counsel stating that they wished time to consider this surprise testimony as he called it, although they had had six months in which to examine it.

If he did not recognize the signature as a forgery in his extended examinations, he was incompetent as a handwriting expert. If he did believe it to be a forgery, he was knowingly assisting in an attempt at a subversion of justice.

A lawyer is entitled to plead his client's cause even though he knows him to be guilty, and it is common practice.

The real scientific expert, however, cannot use his influence to defeat justice without casting reflections on his own ethics and the ethics of his profession.

It was an air-tight case, and the trial judge ruled the last will filed for probate had been proved a forgery. The case was appealed to the State Supreme Court, which upheld the decision in the lower court.

In the meantime, Fred Broesser, the executor, absconded with all the liquid assets of the estate, and a world-wide search was made for him.

He was finally captured in San Francisco as he came down the gangplank of a steamer on which he had secured employment as a pantryman. Broken in health and spirit, he pleaded guilty to betraying his trust, but denied forging the will. In the court room where he had once sat an honored, trusted, and respected officer of the court, he was sentenced to a long term in the Walla Walla Penitentiary.

Thus does life play its inscrutable pranks and humans are left to wonder what imps of ill luck there be that thwart their honest path, or what sinister Nemesis prevails to shadow their evil way.

21
WHY CRIME?

The readers of this volume must be impressed with the futility of a criminal career or even a temporary lapse from the path of social approval. The criminal vainly combats the combined forces of organized existence, of nature, and sometimes, it seems, of even the mysterious influence of Providence. At any rate, the criminal must contend with factors that are beyond his choice or reasoning.

Certain it is that Eddie Whitfield could never have conceived that a needle, fallen from a Douglas fir tree which grew near the road at Battleground, could be the link in a chain of circumstances leading him to the gallows.

Nor could McClurg foresee the fate that planted a sagebrush on Little Freezeout Hill which seemed destined to prevent his hiding his crime. The brush fire that exploded a shell in the discarded gun of a murderer, thus revealing its hiding place, was uncanny in its consequences.

Some would call it retribution, and who can deny? The fear of eternal damnation or the hope of a heavenly reward has always been a deterrent from evil and a stimulant toward the good life. However, in this day of skepticism of the efficacy of religious concepts, their appeal has lost much potency. The criminal often runs amuck because he has neither religious nor moral scruples.

Also he fails to realize that he is an integral part of a well ordered universe, the mysteries of which he cannot comprehend. In disturbing the equilibrium of a harmonious Nature by unsocial acts he brings against himself all the forces that man, a product of nature, has at his disposal.

This concept should be acceptable to everyone of whatever religion or of no religion at all, and would be a powerful substitute for those religious symbols of reward and punishment that are losing their potency in an agnostic age.

After all, our big task as individuals is to chart the course of our life in harmony with nature so as to reap reward and avoid punishment. This is true on the moral or spiritual plane as it is on the physical. Science has worked wonders on the material plane. The late great Thomas Edison observed and learned the secrets of nature and earned the blessings of mankind by translating them to practical uses which have brought comfort to millions. His incandescent lamp is a greater triumph of nature than it is of Edison's inventive genius. And yet, the same lightning that makes electric lights can bring destructive havoc if not understood and controlled by human intelligence.

A greater monument to Mr. Edison than a ten-million-dollar edifice of stone would be the expenditure of such a fund to promote a better understanding of the tremendous significance of human behavior on both moral and physical planes. That would be in accord with the life and accomplishments of this great man.

What the world needs more than anything else is a fixation of moral values on a scientific basis that can be approved by thinking men!

The criminal needs an inner barrier against an unsocial career. The man who thinks he can "get away" with crime is largely deluding himself. Though he may, for a time, escape the hand of the law, he cannot flee his own conscience nor the burning fear of detection and punishment.

In the light of these conditions, why crime, anyway? The man who deliberately commits a crime that may mean a long prison term or death on the gallows is an enigma to the average law-abiding citizen. Why does he do it?

Or, to put it differently, what factors contribute toward developing a murderer and a saint in the same social environments? A German scholar has given us as good an answer as any:

> Why, in one case, the will triumphantly resists these [social] causes, and in another, fails, is an incalculable problem; it is one of those mysteries before which at present we stand baffled with the confession "Ignoramus" on our lips.[1]

Of course, there are many theories and hypotheses, some more significant than others; yet, the workings of the human soul are one of the mysteries of life.

Though I do not propose to enter into a sociological discussion of the source of crime in this concluding chapter, there are a few interesting aspects that may prove thought-provoking to the layman.

One thing is generally admitted. The individual is usually more influenced toward crime by external factors than by inner dispositions that are inherent. Of course, the exception is the pathological case or one who may be congenitally disposed toward some form of crime. He is in the minority.

In this is the greatest hope of repression. If crime were a psychic ailment of the individual in every instance, without contributing causes, repressive measures would be the more difficult to achieve. Inherently the criminal is usually no different from the law-abiding individual. At least, the difference is only a matter of degree.

Criminal tendencies are merely the abuse of praiseworthy qualities of an individual. As was said earlier in this volume, evil may easily be merely an excess of virtue. For instance, acquisitiveness is nature's instinct toward thrift; yet, an excess leads to greed and avarice which breeds crime. A certain amount of belligerency is nature's weapon of self-protection for the individual; but in superabundance it leads to pugnaciousness that may result in crimes of

[1] *Lehrbuch der Gefängnis-kunde*, by Krohne.

violence. Sexual virility and passion is the source of life; but uncontrolled it may bring difficulties. Bravery is a virtue that may be tragic as dare-devil foolhardiness.

From this point of view it would seem that the chief aim of crime repression should be to provide a social environment that would give natural human instincts and emotions a harmless outlet and a creative impulse. The same talents may be either creative or destructive. The playfield, for example, is a well-recognized curative for the mischievous child; as are also recreation and creative work for the energetic adult. This is aside, of course, from the crime deterrent result of punishment and the rehabilitating methods in pathological cases.

If crime is increasing, in accordance with the popular opinion, there is a basic reason for it. It might be supposed that the great advance of civilization would stifle crime as a heritage of savagery. That it does not, puzzles some people, who take a superficial view of the matter and overvalue the regenerative influence of modern life.

I believe that the cramped, artificial mode of living in a highly civilized society warps a great many people and in this way makes a fertile soil for crime of all kinds. The natural instincts and emotions are not given free play in the narrow confines of gregarious society, huddled together in gigantic cities. The love of adventure, the stimulation of dangerous pursuits, the zest of the hunt of wild animals, and so on are all the lot of primitive man. After all, there is much of the savage in each of us, and these atavistic cravings for dangerous adventure find release in some through a career of crime, unless turned into a more useful channel. Just imagine the contentment of a Massasoit poring over the figures of a ledger! How soon would he run amuck!

Sports attempt to meet this need, but after all the majority are in the gallery audiences instead of participating in the games. We are a nation of sports spectators!

The economic status of modern society also has a bearing on the crime problem, as is well known. The saying, "The hungry Indian is a dangerous Indian," is equally true of civilized man. In

many instances it is economic need alone that impels an otherwise normal individual to commit thievery or robbery. An interesting example of this principle has been given by von Mayr:

> In the period from 1835 to 1861, in the Bavarian terri-
> tory, about every half groschen added to the price of grain
> called forth one theft more per 100,000 inhabitants, while
> every half groschen that grain declined in price prevented
> one theft.[2]

Though our own standards of economics today are different,
and adequate statistics are not available, it is, perhaps, safe to assume that certain types of crime increase during periods of depression.

Though civilization has within it the germ of crime because
of a more complex and, in some respects, a more limited mode of
living, it also has within it the hope of a cure—the opportunity for
a greater enlightenment of moral values and the means of altruis-
tic education that can supplant the causes of crime.

Crime repression cannot begin and end with the criminal and
hope to accomplish a full measure of success. This effort must be
broad enough to attack the problem at its source—abject poverty
that breeds desperation and the pathological criminal; a humdrum
existence in a mechanical age that promotes reckless boredom running amuck; the establishing of moral standards based on a conception of a universe that is intolerant of evil and brings its own
punishment.

The individual who is actively employed and who has *learned*
to recognize his own emotional need for amusement and recreation
is rarely tempted into a career of crime. The shadow of a stalking
Nemesis need never cross his path.

---

[2] *Die Gesetzmässigkeit im Gesellschaftsleben* by von Mayr.

Coachwhip Publications

CoachwhipBooks.com

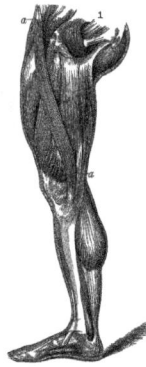

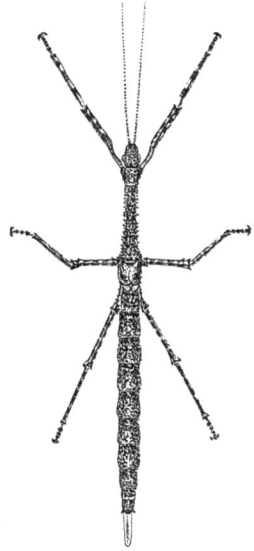

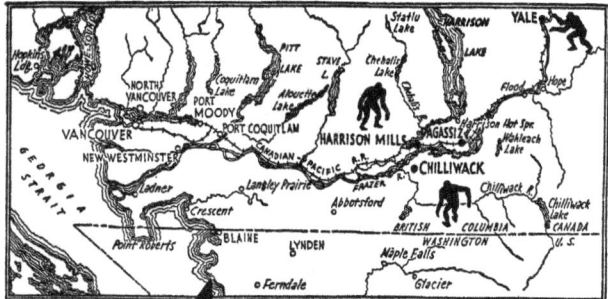

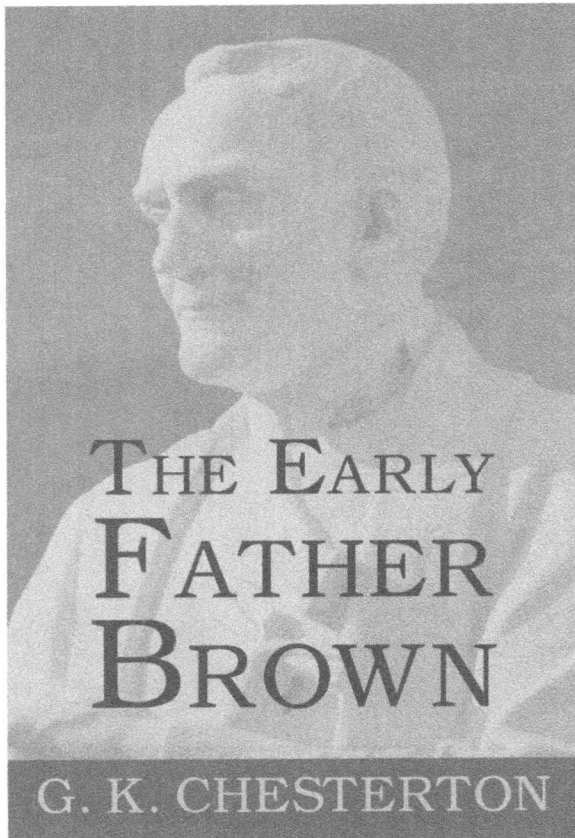

THE EARLY
FATHER
BROWN

G. K. CHESTERTON

THE EARLY FATHER BROWN

ISBN 1-61646-012-1

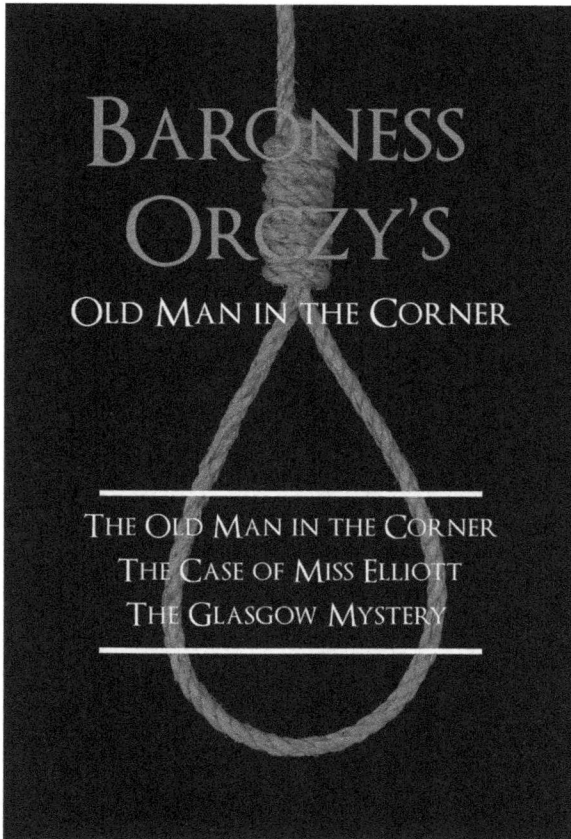

BARONESS ORCZY`S OLD MAN IN THE CORNER

ISBN 1-61646-015-6

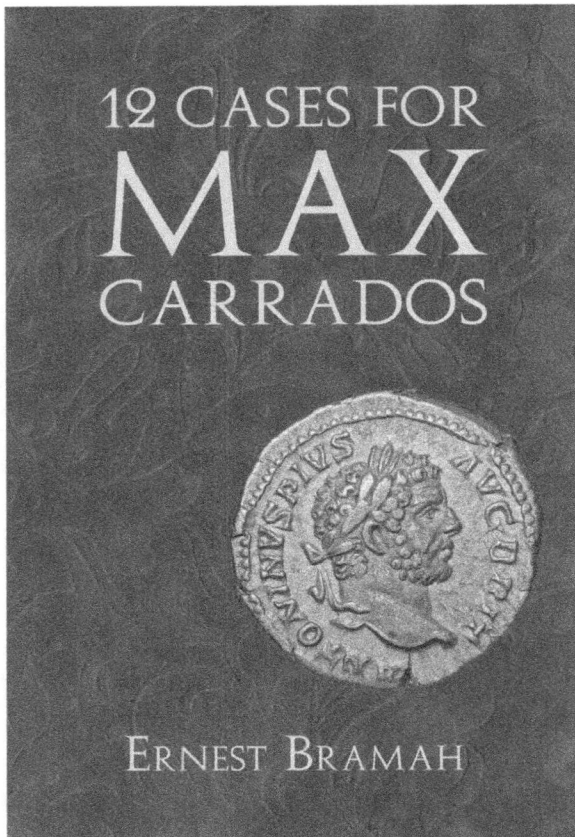

12 CASES FOR **MAX** CARRADOS

ERNEST BRAMAH

12 CASES FOR MAX CARRADOS

ISBN 1-61646-018-0

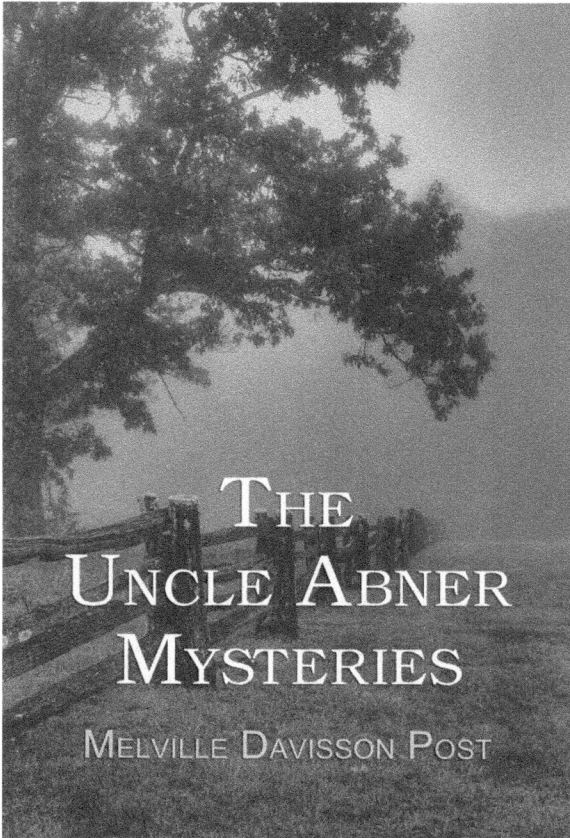

THE UNCLE ABNER MYSTERIES

ISBN 1-61646-016-4

www.ingramcontent.com/pod-product-compliance
Lightning Source LLC
Chambersburg PA
CBHW022335280326
41934CB00006B/639